POEMS TO REMEMBER

LITERARY HERITAGE

ADVISORY EDITORIAL BOARD

LITERATURE TO ENJOY

STORIES TO ENJOY
POEMS TO ENJOY
PLAYS TO ENJOY
READINGS TO ENJOY

LITERATURE TO REMEMBER

STORIES TO REMEMBER
POEMS TO REMEMBER
PLAYS TO REMEMBER
READINGS TO REMEMBER

Revised Edition

POEMS
TO
REMEMBER

DOROTHY PETITT

Professor of English
San Francisco State College
San Francisco, California

THE MACMILLAN COMPANY
COLLIER-MACMILLAN LIMITED   LONDON

ACKNOWLEDGMENTS

For permission to reprint copyright material in this volume, grateful acknowledgment is made to the following:

Atheneum House, Inc.: For "Separation" from *The Moving Target* by W. S. Merwin. Copyright © 1962, 1963 by W. S. Merwin. Reprinted by permission of Atheneum Publishers. For "How to Eat a Poem" by Eve Merriam. Copyright © 1964 by Eve Merriam, from *It Doesn't Always Have to Rhyme*. Used by permission of Atheneum Publishers.

Robert Bly: For "Driving to Town Late to Mail a Letter" and "Love Poem." Copyright 1962 by Robert Bly. Reprinted from *Silence in the Snowy Fields*, (Wesleyan University Press, 1962), by permission of the author.

Arna Bontemps: For "Southern Mansion" by Arna Bontemps from *American Negro Poetry* edited by Arna Bontemps, published by Hill & Wang.

Curtis Brown, Ltd.: For "The Kill" and "The Poem" by Donald Hall. From *A Roof of Tiger Lilies* by Donald Hall. Reprinted by permission.

Jonathan Cape Limited: For "All Day I Hear the Noise of Water" from *Collected Poems* by James Joyce. Reprinted by permission of the Executors of the James Joyce Estate and Jonathan Cape Limited.

Jacques Chambrun, Inc.: For "Ambition" by Morris Bishop from *A Bowl of Bishop* by Morris Bishop.

Chatto and Windus Ltd.: For "For A Lamb" from *Collected Poems* by Richard Eberhart. Reprinted by permission of the publishers, Chatto and Windus Ltd. For "Fishing Harbour Towards Evening" from *Control Tower* by Richard Kell, reprinted by permission of the publishers, Chatto and Windus Ltd.

University of Chicago Press: For "The Picnic" from *Ghosts of the Heart* by John Logan by permission of The University of Chicago Press. Copyright © 1960.

(continued on page 188)

Illustrated by William Hofmann

The Macmillan Company
Collier-Macmillan Canada, Ltd., Toronto, Ontario
Printed in the United States of America

2-K

CONTENTS

2 POEMS EXPRESS IDEAS 24

3 POEMS EXPRESS FEELINGS 44

Seasonal Reflections 46

Love and Loss

6 · SOUNDS SHAPE POEMS

x

7 POEMS MEAN THEMSELVES AND SOMETHING MORE 158

TO THE READER

These are poems for you to remember. After you have read several of them, you may enjoy discovering which ones you remember best.

People remember poems in different ways. Perhaps something vaguely reminds you of a poem you once read. You can't remember the poet, the title of the poem, or even any of the words. You may remember where you read the poem, and you might even try to find it, if the memory is strong enough.

Or, out of nowhere, a line or two of a poem pops into your head. You don't remember the whole poem, just that part. And often you may not know until that unexpected moment that you remember even the part.

Usually you remember an entire poem only if you've made an effort to memorize it. And usually you make an effort to memorize a poem only if you like it so much that you'd like to be able to say it to yourself or to someone else.

May you remember the poems in this book
Because they are new,
Because they are old,
Because the sounds please you,
Because the subjects interest you.

Above all, may you remember the poems in this book because they help you discover what you feel and what you think
About them,
About the world,
About yourself.

1

1
Humor is a Way of Being Serious

All day in school you hear serious statements of very important facts. By night your head is stuffed full. It's almost impossible to remember everything you've heard.

Your science teacher, for example, might require the class to learn the names of the important bones in the human body. While pointing to the bones on his model skeleton, a teacher is likely to pronounce the names carefully in a serious tone of voice. He wants to be sure everyone hears and understands. But even if your classmates hear and understand, would any of them be likely to smile or make jokes about the skeleton? What is humorous about a skeleton, which after all is a very necessary structure? Can you imagine what you would be like without a skeleton?

Many serious statements offer advice. "Study hard, and maybe you'll get a hundred on your bone test tomorrow," your teacher might tell the class as the bell rings. As everyone leaves, the class comic stops to complain. "You mean you're going to test *our* bones? That's not fair; mine are smaller than everyone else's." "That's right," your teacher answers, his mouth not smiling, but his eyes very bright. Would all the listening students be likely to take this conversation seriously? Why or why not?

Sometimes a pal offers you advice. "You know," he might say, "you should always comb your hair that care-free, windblown way. You look so nice and shaggy — just like my uncle's sheep dog." If you hadn't noticed his grin, his poke, or his tone of voice, you might have been hurt or annoyed. But since you know he's friendly, how are you likely to react?

A poet too sometimes makes fun of people's thoughts and actions. Some humorous poems seem to be about animals or other creatures, but the real subject is people. Humor is one way for a poet to be serious, but friendly. He may have a good idea, but he knows that if his readers get annoyed at him, they won't listen. If he makes them laugh, though, maybe they'll consider his idea. They may think about it really seriously. They might even change their ways a little.

Why do you think pals and humorous poets take time to tease people? Do they make fun to hurt or to help? How does the *way* they speak affect your response? Does it help if they seem to be making fun of themselves too?

If a panther should cross your path, what would you do?

THE PANTHER

The panther is like a leopard,
Except it hasn't been peppered.
Should you behold a panther crouch,
Prepare to say Ouch.
Or better yet, if called by a panther,
Don't anther.

—OGDEN NASH

If you have never seen a panther, how might this poem help
you know what he looks like? What other animal would you need
to be acquainted with?
Which rhyme seems most unexpected?
Do you think this poem offers good advice?

► ► ►

THE HIPPOPOTAMUS

I shoot the Hippopotamus
With bullets made of platinum,
Because if I use leaden ones
His hide is sure to flatten 'em.

—HILAIRE BELLOC

► ► ►

A lynx is much like a panther, except that a lynx is smaller.

THE LESSER LYNX

The laughter of the Lesser Lynx
    Is often insincere:
It pays to be polite, he thinks,
    If Royalty is near.

So when the Lion steals his food
    Or kicks him from behind,
He smiles, of course — but oh, the rude
    Remarks that cross his mind!

                                   — E. V. RIEU

How does the Lesser Lynx respond to the Lion's treatment of him? Why does he respond that way?

How is the lynx physically "less" than the lion? Is he "less" than the lion in any other way?

Why might people act like the Lesser Lynx?

Have you ever seen a microbe? What did he look like? If you haven't seen a microbe, how do you know he exists?

THE MICROBE

The Microbe is so very small
You cannot make him out at all,
But many sanguine people hope
To see him through a microscope.
His jointed tongue that lies beneath
A hundred curious rows of teeth;
His seven tufted tails with lots
Of lovely pink and purple spots
On each of which a pattern stands,
    Composed of forty separate bands;
        His eyebrows of a tender green;
            All these have never yet been seen—
                But scientists, who ought to know,
                    Assure us that they must be so . . .
                        Oh! let us never, never doubt
                            What nobody is sure about!

—HILAIRE BELLOC

What does the microbe look like, according to this poem? If he has never yet been seen, how can the poet describe him so completely?

What advice does the poet offer? Are you willing to accept his advice?

Who do you think the poet is making fun of: microbes, scientists, or people who believe everything scientists say?

► ► ►

THE DAYNIGHTLAMP

Korf has a daynightlamp,
His own invention, which
At one flick of the switch,
Turns day, however bright,
To blackest night.

When, at the convention
He displays it on the ramp,
No man of comprehension
Who understands his field
Can fail to see, revealed—

(Brilliant day turns to night;
Applause storms through the house)
(Someone starts to shout
for the janitor, Mr. Camp:
"Lights! Lights!")—to see, outright,

The facts: aforesaid lamp,
Indeed has powers which
At one flick of the switch
Turns any day, how bright,
To blackest night.

—CHRISTIAN MORGENSTERN
(translated by William Snodgrass)

What practical uses can you imagine for a daynightlamp?

Even without such an invention, there might be other ways of turning brightness to darkness. For example, someone might make you sad, when a minute before you were happy. What might he do or say to change your mood?

THE BUS

I was the last passenger of the day,
I was alone on the bus,
I was glad they were spending all that money
just getting me up Eighth Avenue.
Driver! I shouted, it's you and me tonight,
let's run away from this big city
to a smaller city more suitable to the heart,
let's drive past the swimming pools of Miami Beach,
you in the driver's seat, me several seats back,
but in the racial cities we'll change places
so as to show how well you've done up North,
and let us find ourselves some tiny American fishing
      village
in unknown Florida
and park right at the edge of the sand,
a huge bus pointing out,
metallic, painted, solitary,
with New York plates.

—LEONARD COHEN

What gave the bus passenger the idea of running away? Why do you think he wanted to leave New York City?

Why do you think the passenger wants to drive past the swimming pools of Miami Beach? What reason could he have for wanting the bus to park "right at the edge of the sand"?

8

HOW TO EAT A POEM

Don't be polite.
Bite in.
Pick it up with your fingers and lick the juice that
    may run down your chin.
It is ready and ripe now, whenever you are.

You do not need a knife or fork or spoon
or plate or napkin or tablecloth.

For there is no core
or stem
or rind
or pit
or seed
or skin
to throw away.

—EVE MERRIAM

YOU BUY SOME FLOWERS

You buy some flowers for your table;
You tend them tenderly as you're able;
You fetch them water from hither and thither—
What thanks do you get for it all? They wither.

—SAMUEL HOFFENSTEIN

► ► ►

When you were a child, what were your favorite stories? Why did you like them?

DON'T CRY, DARLING, IT'S BLOOD ALL RIGHT

Whenever poets want to give you the idea that something is
    particularly meek and mild,
They compare it to a child,
Thereby proving that though poets with poetry may be
    rife
They don't know the facts of life.
If of compassion you desire either a tittle or a jot,
Don't try to get it from a tot.
Hard-boiled, sophisticated adults like me and you
May enjoy ourselves thoroughly with *Little Women* and
    Winnie-the-Pooh,
But innocent infants these titles from their reading course
    eliminate
As soon as they discover that it was honey and nuts and
    mashed potatoes instead of human flesh that Winnie-
    the-Pooh and Little Women ate.
Innocent infants have no use for fables about rabbits or
    donkeys or tortoises or porpoises,
What they want is something with plenty of well-mutilated
    corpoises.
Not on legends of how the rose came to be a rose instead
    of a petunia is their fancy fed,
But on the inside story of how somebody's bones got
    ground up to make somebody else's bread.
They'll go to sleep listening to the story of the little
    beggarmaid who got to be queen by being kind to
    the bees and the birds,

But they're all eyes and ears the minute they suspect a
   wolf or a giant is going to tear some poor wood-
   cutter into quarters or thirds.
It really doesn't take much to fill their cup;
All they want is for somebody to be eaten up.
Therefore I say unto you, all you poets who are so crazy
   about meek and mild little children and their angelic air,
If you are sincere and really want to please them, why
   just go out and get yourselves devoured by a bear.

                                            —OGDEN NASH

   According to Ogden Nash, what kind of stories appeal to
children? Do you think he is right?
   Do you think Ogden Nash is making fun of children or of
poets? Which lines in the poem make you think so?

                  ► ► ►

STAIRS

Here's to the man who invented stairs
And taught our feet to soar!
He was the first who ever burst
Into a second floor.

The world would be downstairs today
Had he not found the key;
So let his name go down to fame,
Whatever it may be.

                                            —OLIVER HERFORD

"When I Was a Lad" is a song from the operetta, *H. M. S.* (Her Majesty's Ship) *Pinafore*. It is sung by the Right Honorable Sir Joseph Quincy Porter, First Lord of the Admiralty of the British Navy.

WHEN I WAS A LAD
from *H.M.S. Pinafore*

(The chorus is sung by Sir Joseph Porter's ". . . sisters and his cousins,/Whom he reckons up by dozens,/And his aunts." The gallant captain and the crew of the Pinafore also join in.)

When I was a lad I served a term
As office boy to an Attorney's firm.
I cleaned the windows and I swept the floor,
And I polished up the handle on the big front door.
    (Chorus — *He polished up the handle of the big
       front door.)*
I polished up that handle so carefullee
That now I am the Ruler of the Queen's Navee!
    (Ch. — *He polished up that handle so carefullee
       That now he is the Ruler of the Queen's Navee!)*

As office boy I made such a mark
That they gave me the post of a junior clerk.
I served the writs with a smile so bland,
And I copied all the letters in a big round hand.
    (Ch. — *He copied all the letters in a big round hand.)*
I copied all the letters in a hand so free,
That now I am the Ruler of the Queen's Navee!
    (Ch. — *He copied all the letters in a hand so free,
       That now he is the Ruler of the Queen's Navee!)*

In serving writs I made such a name
That an articled clerk I soon became;
I wore clean collars and a brand-new suit
For the pass examination at the Institute.
    (Ch. — *For the pass examination at the Institute.*)
  And that pass examination did so well for me,
  That now I am the Ruler of the Queen's Navee!
    (Ch. — *And that pass examination did so well for he,*
    That now he is the Ruler of the Queen's Navee!)

Of legal knowledge I acquired such a grip
That they took me into the partnership.
And that junior partnership, I ween,
Was the only ship that I ever had seen.
    (Ch. — *Was the only ship that he had ever seen.*)
  But that kind of ship so suited me,
  That now I am the Ruler of the Queen's Navee!
    (Ch. — *But that kind of ship so suited he,*
    That now he is the Ruler of the Queen's Navee!)

I grew so rich that I was sent
By a pocket borough into Parliament.
I always voted at my party's call,
And I never thought of thinking for myself at all.
    (Ch. — *He never thought of thinking for himself at all.*)

I thought so little, they rewarded me
By making me the Ruler of the Queen's Navee!
  (Ch.—*He thought so little, they rewarded he*
  By making him the Ruler of the Queen's Navee!)

Now landsmen all, whoever you may be,
If you want to rise to the top of the tree,
If your soul isn't fettered to an office stool,
Be careful to be guided by this golden rule—
  (Ch.—*Be careful to be guided by this golden rule*—)
Stick close to your desks and never go to sea,
And you all may be Rulers of the Queen's Navee!
  (Ch.—*Stick close to your desks and never go to sea,*
  And you all may be Rulers of the Queen's Navee!)

—W. S. GILBERT

What were the Rt. Hon. Sir Joseph Porter's qualifications to be First Lord of the Admiralty? Which of his experiences do you think best qualified him?

A pocket borough is an old electoral district in which only a few voters are left. Being sent to Parliament by a pocket borough might even mean that you were the only one who voted, and that you had voted for yourself. How does his election fit with the way the Rt. Hon. Sir Joseph Porter behaved after he entered Parliament?

Read all the choruses, one after the other, pretending you don't know the rest of the story. What part of the Lord Admiral's story do the choruses tell? Why do you think the choruses repeat only that part?

Do people sometimes succeed the way the Lord Admiral did? Do you think the writer of this song seriously wants you to follow the Golden Rule of the last stanza?

► ► ►

WHEN YOU'RE AWAY

When you're away, I'm restless, lonely,
Wretched, bored, dejected; only
Here's the rub, my darling dear,
I feel the same when you are near.

—SAMUEL HOFFENSTEIN

▶ ▶ ▶

THE TERMITE

Some primal termite knocked on wood
   And tasted it, and found it good,
And that is why your Cousin May
   Fell through the parlor floor today.

—OGDEN NASH

15

What would be a logical lodging for a toad?

warty bliggens the toad

i met a toad
the other day by the name
of warty bliggens
he was sitting under
a toadstool
feeling contented
he explained that when the cosmos
was created
that toadstool was especially
planned for his personal
shelter from sun and rain
thought out and prepared
for him

do not tell me
said warty bliggens
that there is not a purpose
in the universe
the thought is blasphemy

a little more
conversation revealed
that warty bliggens
considers himself to be
the center of the said
universe
the earth exists
to grow toadstools for him
to sit under
the sun to give him light
by day and the moon
and wheeling constellations
to make beautiful
the night for the sake of
warty bliggens

to what act of yours
do you impute
this interest on the part
of the creator
of the universe
i asked him
why is it that you
are so greatly favored

ask rather
said warty bliggens
what the universe
has done to deserve me
if i were a
human being i would
not laugh
too complacently
at poor warty bliggens
for similar
absurdities
have only too often
lodged in the crinkles
of the human cerebrum

— archy

(DON MARQUIS)

Would you like to meet someone like warty bliggens?

What similarity between human beings and warty did archy see?

According to Don Marquis, archy was a cockroach who used Don Marquis's typewriter to write poems. In the morning, when Mr. Marquis came into the newspaper office where he worked, there in the typewriter would be archy's latest effort.

If you decided only from the punctuation of this poem, would you say archy had been very well educated? Is his vocabulary that of an educated person? Is his understanding of people sound?

Can you judge archy's education on the basis of only one kind of clue? What clues has warty bliggens considered in deciding the purpose of the universe?

► ► ►

AMBITION

I got pocketed behind 7X-3824;
He was making 65, but I can do a little more.
I crowded him on the curves, but I couldn't get past,
And on the straightaways there was always some truck
    coming fast.
Then we got to the top of a mile-long incline
And I edged her out to the left, a little over the white line,
And ahead was a long grade with construction at the bottom,
And I said to the wife, "Now by golly I got'm!"
I bet I did 85 going down the long grade,
And I braked her down hard in front of the barricade,
And I swung in ahead of him and landed fine
Behind 9W-7679.

— MORRIS BISHOP

From the air, what might a freeway look like to a visitor from outer space?

SOUTHBOUND ON THE FREEWAY

A tourist came in from Orbitville,
parked in the air, and said:

The creatures of this star
are made of metal and glass.

Through the transparent parts
you can see their guts.

Their feet are round and roll
on diagrams — or long

measuring tapes — dark
with white lines.

They have four eyes.
The two in the back are red.

Sometimes you can see a 5-eyed
one, with a red eye turning

on the top of his head.
He must be special —

the others respect him,
and go slow,

when he passes, winding
among them from behind.

They all hiss as they glide,
like inches, down the marked

tapes. Those soft shapes,
shadowy inside

the hard bodies — are they
their guts or their brains?

— MAY SWENSON

What did the freeway look like to the visitor from Orbitville?
How would you answer the question at the end? What do you
think caused the tourist to wonder?

▶ ▶ ▶

MONEY

Workers earn it,
Spendthrifts burn it,
Bankers lend it,
Women spend it,
Forgers fake it,
Taxes take it,
Dying leave it,
Heirs receive it,
Thrifty save it,
Misers crave it,
Robbers seize it,
Rich increase it,
Gamblers lose it . . .
I could use it.

— RICHARD ARMOUR

► ► ►

What idea does the Humpty-Dumpty nursery rhyme express?

MOTHER GOOSE
(Circa 2054)

Humpty Dumpty sat on the wall,
A non-electro-magnetic ball.
All the Super's polariscopes
Couldn't revitalize his isotopes.

— IRENE SEKULA

► ► ►

THE EMANCIPATION OF GEORGE-HECTOR

(a coloured turtle)

George-Hector
. . . is
spoiled.
formerly he stayed
well up in his
shell . . . but now
he hangs arms and legs
sprawlingly
in a most langorous fashion . . .
head reared back
to
       be
admired.

he didn't use to talk . . .
but
he does now.

—MARJ EVANS

When might you enjoy having George-Hector around: before
or after his emancipation? What has caused his change?

2

Poems
Express Ideas

"I've got an idea!" someone says. Usually
he's excited when he says it. He might be inspired to
suggest, "Let's have a party!" His idea calls for action:
buying the food and making all other necessary prepara-
tions.

Other ideas don't call quite so clearly for action. In
these ideas, someone seems to say, "That's the way it is,
as I see it." For instance, someone might say, "Good
dancers practice a lot." This idea tells what the speaker
thinks good dancers do, but it doesn't suggest that *you*
practice. Once you've realized the importance of practice,
you can decide for yourself whether or not you're willing
to work to become a good dancer.

To express an idea, a person may tell what some-
thing is like. "The freeway is a rat race," you might say.
Of course, someone else might have a different idea: he
might think it's pleasant to drive on the freeway. What
might the freeway seem like to him?

Where do ideas come from? What happens in your
mind when you get an idea? Maybe something unusual
happens first, or you notice something special or learn
something new. When you react strongly to a happening
or a fact, you wonder what it means. You think about it.
Maybe you think about it for a long time, noticing other

events or facts while you're thinking. The thinking may take a lot of effort, and it may even shake up some of your old ideas.

Then you get your idea. Eureka! A light turns on. Later, after you've investigated and thought some more, you may change your idea. Now, though, you're excited. And you got the idea by yourself.

Poets often get ideas in a similar way. A strong feeling about something might start the poet thinking. Often, in his poem, he'll describe what happened or what he noticed as a background for expressing his idea. Or he may express the idea without telling you what led him to think of it. Then you can imagine what might have caused him to start thinking.

In some poems, poets suggest action. They advise you to do something, but you have to decide for yourself just what to do and when to do it. Do you think that everyone else who reads the poem is likely to make exactly the same decision that you do?

Just as frequently, poems express ideas that say the truth as the poet sees it. Do you necessarily have to agree with his view? However, if you first read his poem carefully to understand his view and then think about it, what might happen in your own mind?

How might a mother persuade her son to stay in school or to stick to a difficult job?

MOTHER TO SON

Well, son, I'll tell you:
Life for me ain't been no crystal stair.
It's had tacks in it,
And splinters,
And boards torn up,
And places with no carpet on the floor —
Bare.
But all the time
I'se been a-climbin' on,
And reachin' landin's
And turnin' corners,
And sometimes goin' in the dark
Where there ain't been no light.
So, boy, don't you turn back.
Don't you set down on the steps
'Cause you finds it kinder hard.
Don't you fall now —
For I'se still goin', honey,
I'se still climbin',
And life for me ain't been no crystal stair.

—LANGSTON HUGHES

What is this mother's advice to her son? What does her advice and the way she gives it show about her?

In what ways has this mother's life not been a "crystal stair"? Imagine a happening that might have been a landing on the stair of her life. What event might have hurt her, in the same way that a tack hurts? Think of other possible happenings for the other things she found on the stair of her life.

For most people, do you think life is likely to be a crystal stair or the kind of stair the mother describes to her son? Which would you prefer your life to be?

► ► ►

Can a certain noise bother you at one time and not even be noticeable at another? What makes the difference in your reaction?

A MINOR BIRD

I have wished a bird would fly away,
And not sing by my house all day;

Have clapped my hands at him from the door
When it seemed as if I could bear no more.

The fault must partly have been in me.
The bird was not to blame for his key.

And of course there must be something wrong
In wanting to silence any song.

—ROBERT FROST

What noise has bothered Robert Frost? What clues in the title and in the poem suggest his reason for not liking the noise?

Why did the poet accept part of the blame for being annoyed? Are people sometimes silenced unfairly? Do you agree with the idea that the last stanza expresses?

THE WILD GEESE LEAVE

Wild geese! I know
that they did eat the barley;
yet, when they go . . .

—YASUI

What do you think will happen when the wild geese go? How are they similar to the minor bird?

We usually think of winter as a dead time of year. But after winter, what season comes?

MORTALITY

This is the surest death
Of all the deaths I know.
The one that halts the breath,
The one that falls with snow
Are nothing but a peace
Before the second zone,
For Aprils never cease
To resurrect their own,
And in my very veins
Flows blood as old as Eve.
The smallest cell contains
Its privileged reprieve.
But vultures recognize
This single mortal thing
And watch with hungry eyes
When hope starts staggering.

—NAOMI LONG MADGETT

How is the death of winter like the death of life? When people die, how might they continue to live on?

According to the poet, what death is the surest of all the deaths she knows? Why might it seem more final than the death of life or the dead season of winter?

How could a person trap moonlight? Why would he want to?

A NET TO SNARE THE MOONLIGHT

(What the Man of Faith Said)

The dew, the rain and moonlight
All prove our Father's mind.
The dew, the rain and moonlight
Descend to bless mankind.

Come, let us see that all men
Have land to catch the rain,
Have grass to snare the spheres of dew,
And fields spread for the grain.

Yea, we would give to each poor man
Ripe wheat and poppies red, —
A peaceful place at evening
With the stars just overhead:

A net to snare the moonlight,
A sod to spread to the sun,
A place of toil by daytime,
Of dreams when toil is done.

—VACHEL LINDSAY

According to the speaker, what do the dew, the rain, and the moonlight all prove? Why do you suppose the poet picked these three things as proof, rather than picking hail, sand, and fire, for instance?

What things does the speaker want all men to have? Why are those things desirable?

What kind of net will snare the moonlight: a real net, like a fish net, or an imaginary one? What connection might a "place of toil by *daytime*" have with a net to snare *moonlight*?

Who is the speaker in this poem? Why do you think the poet made him the speaker? Do you agree with his beliefs?

Suppose the impossible happened, and your body went on vacation for a while, leaving only your head behind. What would you miss being able to do?

GONE AWAY

When my body leaves me
I'm lonesome for it.
I've got

eyes, ears,
nose and mouth
and that's all.

Eyes
keep on seeing the
feather blue of the

cold sky,
mouth takes in
hot soup,
nose

smells the frost,

ears hear everything, all
the noises and absences,
but body

goes away to I don't know where
and it's lonesome to drift
above the space it
fills when it's here.

— DENISE LEVERTOV

How does the poet feel when her body leaves her?

When the poet's body goes away what is left? What are its parts able to do? How can ears hear absences, as well as noises?

This poem expresses an idea directly, but it also hints at an idea indirectly. Can a person's head get along without the rest of his body?

Most people know that mushrooms spring up overnight, but few people know much more than that about the mysterious mushroom.

MUSHROOMS

Overnight, very
Whitely, discreetly,
Very quietly

Our toes, our noses
Take hold on the loam,
Acquire the air.

Nobody sees us,
Stops us, betrays us;
The small grains make room.

Soft fists insist on
Heaving the needles,
The leafy bedding,

Even the paving.
Our hammers, our rams,
Earless and eyeless,

Perfectly voiceless
Widen the crannies,
Shoulder through holes. We

Diet on water,
On crumbs of shadow,
Bland-mannered, asking

Little or nothing.
So many of us!
So many of us!

We are shelves, we are
Tables, we are meek,
We are edible,

Nudgers and shovers
In spite of ourselves.
Our kind multiplies:

We shall by morning
Inherit the earth.
Our foot's in the door.

                                    —SYLVIA PLATH

What facts about mushrooms does Sylvia Plath seem to have
noticed before she wrote this poem?

In what different places does the poem picture mushrooms
growing? Does it matter to them where they grow? What words
in the poem show how mushrooms grow?

How does being a shelf or a table fit with being meek? What
kind of personality do the mushrooms seem to have?

What do the mushrooms seem to be confident of? Do you
think it is likely to happen?

What causes nightmares?

DINKY

O what's the weather in a Beard?
It's windy there, and rather weird,
And when you think the sky has cleared
— Why, there is Dirty Dinky.

Suppose you walk out in a Storm,
With nothing on to keep you warm,
And then step barefoot on a Worm
— Of course, it's Dirty Dinky.

As I was crossing a hot hot Plain,
I saw a sight that caused me pain,
You asked me before,
I'll tell you again:
— It *looked* like Dirty Dinky.

Last night you lay a-sleeping?
No! The room was thirty-five below;
The sheets and blankets turned to snow.
— He'd got in: Dirty Dinky.

You'd better watch the things you do,
You'd better watch the things you do.
You're part of him; he's part of you
— You may be Dirty Dinky.

—THEODORE ROETHKE

What are the scenes in this poem like? What do you imagine
it would feel like to be inside a windy beard? Would you like to
step barefoot on a worm?

Who do *you* think Dirty Dinky is? Do you think the advice
and the idea in the last stanza are sound?

THE REBEL

When I
die
I'm sure
I will have a
Big Funeral . . .
Curiosity
seekers . . .
coming to see
if I
am really
Dead . . .
or just
trying to make
Trouble. . . .

—MARI EVANS

Why is the speaker so sure he'll have a big funeral? Do you agree with him?

► ► ►

when you can't
    get off the ground

flapping your arms
    can be flying

—ROBERT K. HALL

37

Do you think there is a secret of life, one you might find?
Where do you think you might find it written out?

THE SECRET

Two girls discover
the secret of life
in a sudden line of
poetry.

I who don't know the
secret wrote
the line. They
told me

(through a third person)
they had found it
but not what it was
not even

what line it was. No doubt
by now, more than a week
later, they have forgotten
the secret,

the line, the name of
the poem. I love them
for finding what
I can't find,

and for loving me
for the line I wrote,
and for forgetting it
so that

a thousand times, till death
finds them, they may
discover it again, in other
lines

in other
happenings. And for
wanting to know it,
for

assuming there is
such a secret, yes,
for that
most of all.

— DENISE LEVERTOV

Why does the poet love the girls? Which reason do you think is the best one?

Think of lines of poetry you especially like. Do they seem to contain the secret of life? If you don't think they contain the secret of life, can you say what they do contain for you?

Judging from this poem, do you think your favorite lines necessarily mean the same thing to the poet who wrote them as they do to you? Would the writer of the lines like the meaning you find in them?

How does "The Secret" look like a poem? How is its appearance on the page different from some of the poems you have read?

What repetitions help connect the words of the poem to each other?

► ► ►

Can a poem last forever? Can a person be forever young?

BLUE GIRLS

Twirling your blue skirts, traveling the sward
Under the towers of your seminary,
Go listen to your teachers old and contrary
Without believing a word.

Tie the white fillets then about your lustrous hair
And think no more of what will come to pass
Than bluebirds that go walking on the grass
And chattering on the air.

Practice your beauty, blue girls, before it fail;
And I will cry with my loud lips and publish
Beauty which all our power shall never establish,
It is so frail.

For I could tell you a story which is true:
I know a lady with a terrible tongue,
Blear eyes fallen from blue,
All her perfections tarnished — and yet it is not long
Since she was lovelier than any of you.

                                   —JOHN CROWE RANSOM

The girls in this poem probably all wore blue skirts as a
school uniform. Does this poet believe the beauty of the blue
girls will last?

What does the poet compare them to? In what ways is that
comparison appropriate? What are the main colors in the picture
of the girls? Taken all together, do the details of the description
paint a happy or sad picture?

40

What does the poet advise the girls to do? What does he say he will do? How is he keeping his promise by writing the poem? Do you think this poet is sad at what he fears might happen? Do you think he wants the girls to think about what could happen to them? Is there any way the girls can avoid the fate of the lady with the terrible tongue?

► ► ►

What do you think makes a suitable subject for a poem?

AMERICAN POETRY

Whatever it is, it must have
A stomach that can digest
Rubber, coal, uranium, moons, poems.

Like the shark, it contains a shoe.
It must swim for miles through the desert
Uttering cries that are almost human.

—LOUIS SIMPSON

What kind of stomach could digest rubber, coal, uranium, moons, poems, and shoes? Do you know poems that discuss those subjects or similar ones?

How can anyone or anything swim through a desert? When Mr. Simpson says a poem "must swim," how is he saying it must move? What kind of readers would be like a desert for a poem?

What kinds of sounds do the poems you have read make? How do those cries seem "almost" human? Can a poem ever sound exactly like human experience?

► ► ►

Can you name a human king who will rule forever?

NAME US A KING

Name us a king
who shall live forever—
a peanut king, a potato king,
a gasket king, a brass-tack king,
a wall-paper king with a wall-paper crown
and a wall-paper queen with wall-paper jewels.

Name us a king
so keen, so fast, so hard,
he shall last forever—
and all the yes-men square shooters
telling the king, "Okay Boss, you shall
    last forever! and then some!"
telling it to an onion king, a pecan king,
a zipper king or a chewing gum king,
any consolidated amalgamated syndicate king—
listening to the yes-men telling him
he shall live forever, he is so keen,
    so fast, so hard,
an okay Boss who shall never bite the dust,
never go down and be a sandwich for the worms
    like us—the customers,
    like us—the customers.

                                    —CARL SANDBURG

What is the idea this poem expresses? Why do you think Mr.
Sandburg didn't say the idea in the poem?

3
Poems
Express Feelings

Every year the cycle of the seasons repeats itself. The freshness of spring is followed by the fullness of long summer days. Then comes the harvest of fall, succeeded by the still cold of winter. Life, we know, has not gone, but has only withdrawn until spring allows it to come forth again.

Sometimes we get so used to having the seasons come and go that we forget to notice them. Yet, whether we are aware of them or not, they are there, partly influencing our moods. A beautiful spring day can make us feel carefree and full of hope. A hot summer day might make us feel lazy. Fall may bring emotions as varied as the weather. How are you likely to feel on a cold, gray winter day?

The ancient Greeks saw the changes of the seasons and wondered at them. Their story of Persephone, a beautiful maiden, explains how the seasons came to be.

One day while she was picking wild flowers, Persephone was stolen by the lord of the underworld and taken to his dark kingdom of death. There she grieved, while on earth her mother, Demeter, the goddess of the corn and other grain, also grieved. Soon the land was barren and desolate like the mother's grief. Zeus, the ruler of the gods, realized that he must act, or men would die of hunger.

Zeus made a bargain with Demeter. Persephone would be held in the underworld for the winter months of the year. In return, Demeter would give grain to the fields again. Thus Persephone returned to the earth, her return bringing renewed life after the darkness of barren winter. And thus she returns every spring.

Ever since, men have seen in the seasons a miniature picture of the longer cycle of human life. As spring flowers may remind us that their beauty cannot last, so youth may remind us that it will grow old and die.

Rather than being sad because beauty and youth are temporary, we enjoy them all the more while we have them. We know that all human beings are mortal and will someday die. That knowledge makes human life and human love even more precious. Poets celebrate the experience of love in poem after poem.

When death does come, we are sad, but not surprised. Life, like the seasons, goes on though an individual life has stopped. The living remember the person who has died as he was in life. A poet expresses his sorrow by writing about the way someone lived. His poem, called an elegy, is really a love poem, expressing wonder at the gift of life.

Seasonal Reflections

What tells you spring has come? How do you feel when you see signs of spring?

VERNAL SENTIMENT

Though the crocuses poke up their heads in the usual
    places,
The frog scum appear on the pond with the same froth of
    green,
And boys moon at girls with last year's fatuous faces,
I never am bored, however familiar the scene.

When from under the barn the cat brings a similar litter,—
Two yellow and black, and one that looks in between,—
Though it all happened before, I cannot grow bitter:
I rejoice in the spring, as though no spring ever had been.

                           —THEODORE ROETHKE

How does Theodore Roethke feel about the signs of spring he sees? Why do you think he feels that way? In all the signs of spring, what is happening?

A daffodil is sometimes called a narcissus. In Greek legend, the youth Narcissus became a flower when he was drowned trying to reach the reflection of his own handsome face.

DAFFODILS

Yellow telephones
in a row in the garden
are ringing,
shrill with light.

Old-fashioned spring
brings earliest models out
each April the same,
naive and classical.

Look into the yolk—
colored mouthpieces
alert with echoes.
Say hello to time.

—MAY SWENSON

How is spring a topsy-turvy time?

because it's

Spring
thingS

dare to do people

(& not
the other way

round)because it

's A
pril

Lives lead their own

persons(in
stead
of everybodyelse's)but

what's wholly
marvellous my

Darling

is that you &
i are more than you

& i(be

ca
us

e It's we)

What kinds of things happen because it's spring?
How does life sometimes seem to lead a person? Could any-
one else be led in the same way? What spring feeling makes
the *you* and *i* of the poem more than *you* and *i*?
Notice the capitalization and the parentheses in this poem.
Notice also the way lines of the poem are printed. How does the
appearance of the poem fit the description of spring?

► ► ►

Spring dawn:
Turning toward the storm cloud,
I lost sight of the bird.

—JULIUS LESTER

49

After lunch in the fields on a hot midsummer day, what might a farmer feel like doing?

MIDSUMMER PAUSE

There is a moment in midsummer when the earth
pauses between flower and fruit; the hay is cut,
the oats ripen, on pasture knolls pearly everlasting
lifts its small fountains of silver and gold.

The skies are blue, the hills rest all day
like men at noon under a shady tree.
The leaves have turned dark green, they hoard
their strength, no strong wind harms them.
Boys swim under the big elm by the crick.
Locusts drone in the trees; the swallows
gather on wires, and starlings in flocks
wheel over the meadows like curving hands.

—FRED LAPE

How do you think it would feel to be alive on this midsummer day? What work needs to be done?

How does the description of the fields help you to feel the mood of the day? The everlasting plant has flowers which keep their shape and color when dried. Why do you think the poet chose to describe the flowers of the everlasting in detail? What does he indirectly compare the plant to?

How do the descriptions of the hills and the trees fit the mood of the day? What *is* happening on this day? What word imitates a sound? Does that sound come every once in a while, or does it go on and on?

Using both the verb and the comparison which show their motion, imagine how the starlings would look flying. How does the way they fly fit the mood of the day?

SUMMER HAIKU

For Frank and Marian Scott

Silence

and a deeper silence

when the crickets

hesitate

—LEONARD COHEN

51

In the fall, what causes apples to ripen? What happens to the apples when they ripen?

CRABAPPLES

Sweeten these bitter wild crabapples, Illinois October sun. The roots here came from the wilderness, came before man came here. They are bitter as the wild is bitter.

Give these crabapples your softening gold, October sun, go through to the white wet seeds inside and soften them black. Make these bitter apples sweet. They want you, sun.

The drop and the fall, the drop and the fall, the apples leaving the branches for the black earth under, they know you from last year, the year before last, October sun.

—CARL SANDBURG

Who do you think is speaking in this poem? Who is he talking to? Why do you suppose he takes the trouble to speak? Won't the sun shine and the apples ripen without his encouragement?

What repeated words and phrases linger in your mind? How is the warmth of the October sun a repetition?

► ► ►

What mood can you feel on a fall night?

FALL WIND

Pods of summer crowd around the door;
I take them in the autumn of my hands.

Last night I heard the first cold wind outside;
and wind blew soft, and yet I shiver twice:

Once for thin walls, once for the sound of time.

—WILLIAM STAFFORD

How does the fall wind make the poet feel?
What plants have pods in the fall? What are the pods like? Are they beautiful? Do they still hold seeds?
Why do you think the poet's hands might be like autumn? How many times did the poet shiver? What or who has thin walls? How can you hear the sound of time? Why do you think he didn't keep on shivering?

When do wild geese fly south? What pattern do they make against the sky?

Wild geese flying
In stiff, stiff lines —
The sky colder.

—SUIHA

53

What would autumn leaves, falling, sound like?

NOVEMBER NIGHT

Listen . . .
With faint dry sound,
Like steps of passing ghosts,
The leaves, frost-crisp'd, break from the trees
And fall.

— ADELAIDE CRAPSEY

► ► ►

Not all monkeys live in the tropics. Some live in Japan, which
has all the seasons, including winter.

First winter rain;
The monkey also seems to wish
For a small straw rain-coat.

— BASHO

What expression on a monkey's face might make him seem
to wish for a raincoat? Who else might "also" wish for one?

► ► ►

54

In traditional Japanese houses, the doors are sliding paper screens, covered by heavy wooden shutters in winter.

The winter fly
Weakly collides
With the sliding doors.

—ANONYMOUS

What is the mood of winter, as this haiku describes it?

If you were limited to only a few things to picture winter, which ones would you choose?

WINTER

Now the snow
lies on the ground
and more snow
is descending upon it—
Patches of red dirt
hold together
the old snow patches

This is winter—
rosettes of
leather-green leaves
by the old fence
and bare trees
marking the sky—

This is winter
winter, winter
leather-green leaves
spearshaped
in the falling snow

—WILLIAM CARLOS WILLIAMS

What things picture winter to William Carlos Williams? Why do you think he says *winter* three times in the last stanza?

What are the colors of winter? What are the shapes of the old snow and the red dirt? Of the leaves together? Of the leaves separately? What kind of marks do bare trees make against the sky?

What is the mood of winter, as this poem pictures it?

► ► ►

"MOUNTAINS AND PLAINS"

Mountains and plains,
   all are captured by the snow —
      nothing remains.

—JŌSŌ

► ► ►

IN THE BLUE

In the blue
a bank of black birds
that shriek, flutter, and alight
on a stiff poplar tree.
In the naked grove
the grave quiet jackdaws
write cold black notes
on February staffs.

—ANTONIO MACHADO
(translated by Willis Barnstone)

Love and Loss

When do you think a young man is old enough to begin loving a young lady?

BROWN PENNY

I whispered, "I am too young."
And then, "I am old enough";
Wherefore I threw a penny
To find out if I might love.
"Go and love, go and love, young man,
If the lady be young and fair."
Ah, penny, brown penny, brown penny,
I am looped in the loops of her hair.

O love is the crooked thing,
There is nobody wise enough
To find out all that is in it,
For he would be thinking of love
Till the stars had run away
And the shadows eaten the moon.
Ah, penny, brown penny, brown penny,
One cannot begin it too soon.

—WILLIAM BUTLER YEATS

Why did the young man toss a penny? When does he decide to begin to love? Do you think his decision is wise?

Why do you think the poet talks about stars, shadows, and the moon in this poem, rather than talking about blue skies and sun? According to the poem, is love simple or complicated? How likely is it that someone could completely understand love?

What repeated words and phrases sing in your mind after you hear the poem? Does the repetition sound happy or sad?

▶ ▶ ▶

A PROVERB

Before you love,
Learn to run through snow
Leaving no footprint.

—POWYS MATHERS
(translated from the Turkish)

To what might you compare someone you love?

MY STAR

All that I know
 Of a certain star
Is, it can throw
 (Like the angled spar)
Now a dart of red,
 Now a dart of blue;
Till my friends have said
 They would fain see, too
My star that dartles the red and the blue!
Then it stops like a bird; like a flower, hangs furled:
 They must solace themselves with the Saturn above it.
What matter to me if their star is a world?
 Mine has opened its soul to me; therefore I love it.

—ROBERT BROWNING

Who do you think Robert Browning's star is?

A spar is a mineral which reflects light, as a crystal does. How does red light make things look? How does blue? What feelings might each kind of light stand for? What kind of star might send out both kinds of light?

Solace means to comfort. Why do the friends need to comfort themselves?

What do the comparisons suggest about the star's nature? Why does the poet prefer his star to a world?

► ► ►

THE PLANTER'S DAUGHTER

When night stirred at sea
And the fire brought a crowd in,
They say that her beauty
Was music in mouth
And few in the candlelight
Thought her too proud,
For the house of the planter
Is known by the trees.

Men that had seen her
Drank deep and were silent,
The women were speaking
Wherever she went—
As a bell that is rung
Or a wonder told shyly,
And O she was the Sunday
In every week.

—AUSTIN CLARKE

What was the beauty of the planter's daughter like? What does each comparison suggest about the sound of her voice? What does each suggest about her character?

How did other people react to her? Why do you think men's reactions were different from women's?

If you were painting a portrait of the planter's daughter, what would you have her doing? Might the background for her portrait include trees? What kind of trees?

► ► ►

When might a boy and a girl discover each other?

THE PICNIC

It is the picnic with Ruth in the spring.
Ruth was third on my list of seven girls
But the first two were gone (Betty) or else
Had someone (Ellen has accepted Doug).
Indian Gully the last day of school;
Girls make the lunches for the boys too.
I wrote a note to Ruth in algebra class
Day before the test. She smiled, and nodded.
We left the cars and walked through the young corn
The shoots green as paint and the leaves like tongues
Trembling. Beyond the fence where we stood
Some wild strawberry flowered by an elm tree

And Jack-in-the-pulpit was olive ripe.
A blackbird fled as I crossed, and showed
A spot of gold or red under its quick wing.
I held the wire for Ruth and watched the whip
Of her long, striped skirt as she followed.
Three freckles blossomed on her thin, white back
Underneath the loop where the blouse buttoned.
We went for our lunch away from the rest,
Stretched in the new grass, our heads close
Over unknown things wrapped up in wax papers.
Ruth tried for the same, I forgot what it was,
And our hands were together. She laughed,
And a breeze caught the edge of her little
Collar and the edge of her brown, loose hair
That touched my cheek. I turned my face in-
to the gentle fall. I saw how sweet it smelled.
She didn't move her head or take her hand.
I felt a soft caving in my stomach
As at the top of the highest slide
When I had been a child, but was not afraid,
And did not know why my eyes moved with wet
As I brushed her cheek with my lips and brushed
Her lips with my own lips. She said to me
Jack, Jack, different than I had ever heard,
Because she wasn't calling me, I think,
Or telling me. She used my name to
Talk in another way I wanted to know.
She laughed again and then she took her hand;
I gave her what we both had touched — can't
Remember what it was, and we ate the lunch.
Afterward we walked in the small, cool creek
Our shoes off, her skirt hitched, and she smiling,
My pants rolled, and then we climbed up the high
Side of Indian Gully and looked

Where we had been our hands together again.
It was then some bright thing came in my eyes,
Starting at the back of them and flowing
Suddenly through my head and down my arms
And stomach and my bare legs that seemed not
To stop in feet, not to feel the red earth
Of the gully, as though we hung in a
Touch of birds. There was a word in my throat
With the feeling and I knew the first time
What it meant and I said, it's beautiful.
Yes, she said, and I felt the sound and word
In my hand join the sound and word in hers
As in one name said, or in one cupped hand.
We put back on our shoes and socks and we
Sat in the grass awhile, crosslegged, under
A blowing tree, not saying anything.
And Ruth played with shells she found in the creek,
As I watched. Her small wrist which was so sweet
To me turned by her breast and the shells dropped
Green, white, blue, easily into her lap,
Passing light through themselves. She gave the pale
Shells to me, and got up and touched her hips
With her light hands, and we walked down slowly
To play the school games with the others.

—JOHN LOGAN

How had Jack happened to ask Ruth to go with him to the picnic? What does Jack remember about how the picnic-place and Ruth looked?

What does he remember about the lunch? Why do you think he remembers some things so well and others so vaguely?

Afterward, how did the creek feel? Why do you think they looked back at where they had been? What was beautiful? How were the sound of the word and its meaning joined?

How clearly does Jack remember Ruth playing with the shells? How is the way the shells react to light like Jack's discovery on the side of Indian Gully?

How did the experience end? Do you think it is an appropriate ending?

► ► ►

LOVE POEM

When we are in love, we love the grass,
And the barns, and the lightpoles,
And the small mainstreets abandoned all night.

—ROBERT BLY

How do you feel when you get a telephone call from someone you like very much?

your little voice
                Over the wires came leaping
and i felt suddenly
dizzy
        With the jostling and shouting of merry flowers
wee skipping high-heeled flames
courtesied before my eyes
                        or twinkling over to my side
Looked up
with impertinently exquisite faces
floating hands were laid upon me
I was whirled and tossed into delicious dancing
up
Up
with the pale important
                        stars and the Humorous
                                                moon
dear girl
How i was crazy how i cried when i heard
                        over time
and tide and death
leaping
Sweetly
        your voice
                                —E. E. CUMMINGS

How did hearing the girl's voice on the telephone make the poet feel?

How can flowers shout? What kind of flames might seem to be wearing high heels? What do the flames seem to be doing? Why do you think the poet chose flowers and flames to picture his feeling?

What was his journey to the stars and moon like?

Can anyone get there directly yet, even on a rocket-ship? Why do stars seem pale to us? How are they important? In what way can the moon be humorous? Why do you think her voice sent him to this kind of stars and to this kind of moon?

At the beginning of the poem, Cummings says her voice came leaping over the wires. At the end, what does he say it came leaping over? How could telephone wires seem to become those things?

Why do you think Mr. Cummings expressed his feelings without putting any periods in? How does the shape of the poem on the page help express his feelings?

► ► ►

THE COLORADO TRAIL

Eyes like the morning star,
  Cheek like a rose,
Laura was a pretty girl,
  God Almighty knows.

Weep, all ye little rains,
  Wail, winds, wail,
All along, along, along
  The Colorado trail.

—AMERICAN FOLK SONG

67

On returning to his home town after a long absence, how might a modern soldier feel?

SOLDIER'S SONG

I joined the army when I was fifteen,
I returned only when my hair was gray.
On the way I met some villagers.
I asked them who was living in my home.
"Far away, over there is your house.
Tombs are built among the pine trees.
The rabbits run in and out of the dog holes,
And pheasants are flying from the roof beams.
In the courtyard grow the wild rice shoots;
The sweet ferns flourish by the wellside."
I cook rice in the grain,
And prepare a soup of ferns.
As soon as dinner is ready,
I do not know who to call.
When I stagger out and look to the east,
Tears fall and wet my clothes.

—CHINESE HAN POEM
(translated by Ho Yung)

How has this Chinese soldier's home changed?
What details do the villagers use to describe the condition of the soldier's house? What words can you think of to sum up his feelings?

► ► ►

In his autobiography, Issa describes his feelings after the death of his small daughter:

For myself—I knew well it was no use to cry, that water once flown past the bridge does not return, and blossoms that are scattered are gone beyond recall. Yet try as I would, I could not, simply could not cut the binding cord of human love.

He then wrote this haiku to express his feelings:

The world of dew
Is the world of dew,
And yet . . .
And yet . . .

—ISSA

Why do you think Issa wrote about dew in his haiku? How might a little girl's life be like dew?
What is Issa reminding himself of in his haiku? Why do you think he doesn't finish his statement?

► ► ►

French soldiers and sailors were sent to Mexico in the 1860's to fight against Juarez's Mexican reform government set up in Vera Cruz. There, many of them died of fever.

LETTER FROM MEXICO
(Vera Cruz, 10 February, 186–)

You entrusted the boy to me. He has died
Along with his comrades, poor young soul. The crew —
There is no more crew; and whether the last few
Of us see France again, fate will decide.

No role a man can choose becomes him more
Than the sailor's. Perhaps it is for this
That landsmen resent him: that they do is sure.
Think what a hard apprenticeship it is.

I weep to write this, I, old Leather-Face.
Death is indifferent to what hide he tans;
Would God he'd taken mine in the lad's place.
Yet this was not my fault nor any man's;

The fever strikes like clock-work; someone falls
Each hour. The cemetery sets a ration —
Which place my sergeant (a Parisian) calls,
After his zoo, *le jardin d'acclimatation.*

Console yourself. Life crushes men like flies.
— In his sea-bag were these trophies: a girl's face,
Two little slippers, probably the size
"For his sister," as the note inside one says.

He sent his mother word: that he had prayed;
His father: that he would have liked some bolder
Death, in battle. At the last two angels stayed
Beside him there. A sailor. An old soldier.

—WILLIAM MEREDITH
(translated from Tristan Corbière)

Who is writing this letter? What has been his relationship to the boy? What does the way he writes show you about him? For instance, is he proud to be a sailor? Has his hard life toughened him?

In France, a zoo is called *Le jardin d'acclimatation* (the garden of acclimatization) because the wild animals must adjust to a different climate and to a different kind of life in order to survive. What might the sergeant have meant when he called the cemetery a place of survival?

What do the trophies in his seabag suggest about the boy's character? What do his messages suggest?

How do you think the boy's parents felt, reading this letter?

▶ ▶ ▶

How might a teacher feel about the accidental death of a student?

ELEGY FOR JANE
(My student, thrown by a horse)

I remember the neckcurls, limp and damp as tendrils;
And her quick look, a sidelong pickerel smile;
And how, once startled into talk, the light syllables leaped
    for her,
And she balanced in the delight of her thought,
A wren, happy, tail into the wind,
Her song trembling the twigs and small branches.
The shade sang with her;
The leaves, their whispers turned to kissing;
And the mold sang in the bleached valleys under the rose.

Oh, when she was sad, she cast herself down into such a
    pure depth,
Even a father could not find her:
Scraping her cheek against straw;
Stirring the clearest water.

My sparrow, you are not here,
Waiting like a fern, making a spiny shadow.
The sides of wet stones cannot console me,
Nor the moss, wound with the last light.

If only I could nudge you from this sleep,
My maimed darling, my skittery pigeon.
Over this damp grave I speak the words of my love:
I, with no rights in this matter,
Neither father nor lover.

—THEODORE ROETHKE

What does this poet-teacher remember about his student?

What do the comparisons suggest to you about how Jane looked, talked, and moved? Was she always happy?

What repetitions of sounds make patterns especially pleasing to your ears? Which adjectives help give you a very clear picture of the nouns they describe?

Why do you think the teacher talks directly to Jane in the last two stanzas?

► ► ►

Think of a man you consider great. What would you compare
him to?

a great

man
is
gone.

Tall as the truth

was who:and
wore his(mountains
understand

how)life

like a(now
with
one sweet sun

in it, now with a

million
flaming billion kinds
of nameless

silence)sky;

                                        —E. E. CUMMINGS

According to the poem, how tall was the great man? How tall is that? What was the way the great man lived ("wore his life") like? Why do you think the poet said, "wore his life," rather than "lived"? What do mountains and the great man have in common? What happening or feeling might be an actual "sweet sun" in the life of a great man? Why do you think the poet says there was only one sun at a time?

Think of silences you have heard. Have any been full of meaning? What kind of silence could be described as "flaming"? How many silences had there been in the great man's life? What happenings might cause the silences?

In 1955, when Emmett Till was fifteen, he left his hometown of Chicago to visit relatives in Greenwood, Mississippi. There he was beaten and shot by two white men because, one of them claimed, Emmett had insulted his wife. Both men were acquitted of murder.

THE LAST QUATRAIN OF THE BALLAD OF EMMETT TILL

after the murder,
after the burial
Emmett's mother is a pretty-faced thing;
    the tint of pulled taffy.
She sits in a red room,
    drinking black coffee.
She kisses her killed boy.
    And she is sorry.
Chaos in windy grays
    through a red prairie.

—GWENDOLYN BROOKS

75

4
Poems
Tell Stories

Poems tell both long stories and short ones. Many long stories are told in folk songs, which may once have been even longer than the versions we have today. In being handed down orally from generation to generation, the less important parts of the stories have often been left out. Though still relatively long, the songs have become shorter, as a beach pebble is rubbed smaller and smoother by the constant action of the waves.

Sometimes poets write poems imitating the folk songs, but there are usually differences between a literary ballad and an authentic one. For one thing, you know who the author of a literary ballad is, but the author of a folk song wrote his poem so long ago that he is anonymous to us today. How else might you be able to tell the difference between a folk ballad and a literary ballad?

Whether written by a known or an unknown author, a long story has the advantage of being able to tell you more than a short story can. A long poem can tell a person's whole life story, or it can tell one significant experience in great detail. In either case, a poem tells a long story as an illustration of some important truth about life. The narrative, we say, has a point.

A short narrative poem has a point too. You usually get to the point quickly, as when you listen to a joke. But in either long or short narrative poems, the point won't always be expressed as obviously as it is in punch lines of most jokes. Poems often don't say the point in so many words. Instead, you have to think about the story in order to understand its meaning. Even when you understand, often you will find it difficult to state the point.

The meaning of a story lies partly in what happens, partly in how it is told, partly in how it turns out. For example, according to an old saying, all the world loves a lover. But lovers do not necessarily have to live happily ever after to interest the world. When a love story doesn't end happily (and some of the best ones don't), at least one of the lovers has to be admirable for some reason. It's even better if both of them are.

All the world loves courage too, even if it's not successful. Many poems tell stories of brave men who did gallant deeds. If a poem tells a man's entire life story, it is bound to end with death, because that's the way life ends. What matters in such a story is not that a brave man has died, but that he has lived.

THE WRAGGLE TAGGLE GYPSIES, O!

Three Gypsies stood at the castle-gate,
They sang so high, they sang so low;
The lady sat in her chamber late,
Her heart it melted away as snow.

They sang so sweet, they sang so shrill,
That fast her tears began to flow.
And she laid down her silken gown,
Her golden rings and all her show.

She pluck-ed off her high-heeled shoes,
A-made of Spanish leather, O.
She would in the street, with her bare, bare feet;
All out in the wind and weather, O.

"O saddle to me my milk-white steed,
And go and fetch me my pony, O!
That I may ride and seek my bride,
Who is gone with the wraggle taggle Gypsies, O!"

O he rode high, and he rode low,
He rode through wood and copses too,
Until he came to an open field,
And there he espied his a-lady, O!

"What makes you leave your house and land?
Your golden treasures for to go?
What makes you leave your new-wedded lord,
To follow the wraggle taggle Gypsies, O?"

"What care I for my house and my land?
What care I for my treasure, O?
What care I for my new-wedded lord,
I'm off with the wraggle taggle Gypsies, O!"

"Last night you slept on a goose-feather bed,
With the sheet turned down so bravely, O!
And tonight you'll sleep in a cold open field,
Along with the wraggle taggle Gypsies, O!"

"What care I for a goose-feather bed,
With the sheet turned down so bravely, O!
For tonight I shall sleep in a cold open field,
Along with the wraggle taggle Gypsies, O!"

— ENGLISH BALLAD

What did this bride give up to go with the gypsies? What won
her from her new-wedded lord?

If you were going to plan a dance or a skit based on this
ballad, into what scenes would you divide the action?

Who would speak in each scene of the skit? What might
dancers be doing during each scene?

This traditional song is so old that no one knows when it was
first sung. What kinds of repetition help to make the story
memorable?

There are many different versions of this song, but in all the
versions the basic story remains the same. The wealthy bride
runs off with a gypsy or gypsies. Why do you suppose many
generations have found this plot appealing?

► ► ►

In times past, the younger daughter in a family could marry only after her elder sister had been wooed and won.

THE TWO SISTERS OF BINNORIE

There were two sisters sat in a bower;
Binnorie, O Binnorie;
There came a knight to be their wooer;
By the bonny mill-dams of Binnorie.

He courted the eldest with gloves and rings,
But he loved the youngest above all things.

The eldest was vexèd to despair,
And much she envied her sister fair.

The eldest said to the youngest one,
"Will ye see our father's ships come in?"

She's taken her by the lily-white hand,
And led her down to the river strand.

The youngest stood upon a stone;
The eldest came and pushed her in.

"O sister, sister, reach your hand,
And you shall be heir of half my land.

"O sister, reach me but your glove
And sweet William shall be all your love."

"Sink on, nor hope for hand or glove!
Sweet William shall surely be my love."

Sometimes she sank, sometimes she swam,
Until she came to the mouth of the dam.

Out then came the miller's son
And saw the fair maid swimming in.

"O father, father, draw your dam!
Here's either a mermaid or a swan."

The miller hasted and drew his dam,
And there he found a drowned woman.

You could not see her middle small,
Her girdle was so rich withal.

You could not see her yellow hair
For the gold and pearls that clustered there.

And by there came a harper fine
Who harped to nobles when they dine.

And when he looked that lady on,
He sighed and made a heavy moan.

He's made a harp of her breast bone,
Whose sounds would melt a heart of stone.

He's taken three locks of her yellow hair
And with them strung his harp so rare.

He went into her father's hall
To play his harp before them all.

But as he laid it on a stone,
The harp began to play alone.

And soon the harp sang loud and clear,
"Farewell, my father and mother dear.

Farewell, farewell, my brother Hugh,
Farewell, my William, sweet and true."

And then as plain as plain could be,
   Binnorie, O Binnorie
"There sits my sister who drownèd me
   By the bonny mill-dams of Binnorie!"

—ENGLISH BALLAD

Why did the elder drown her sister? What do you think became of the elder sister?

Could a harp, even one made of a drowned maiden's breastbone, really play by itself? Could the elder sister have thought it did? Why might she have thought so?

Who is the heroine of "The Two Sisters of Binnorie"? What makes her a heroine?

In the troubled times of the past, many rebel outlaws defied the rule of kings. Yet, as men of honor themselves, they trusted the word of kings.

JOHNIE ARMSTRONG

There dwelt a man in faire Westmerland,
    Johnie Armstrong men did him call,
He had nither lands nor rents coming in,
    Yet he kept eight score men in his hall.

He had horse and harness for them all,
    Goodly steeds were all milke-white;
O the golden bands an about their necks,
    And their weapons, they were all alike.

Newes then was brought unto the king
    That there was sicke a won as hee,   (*such*)
That lived lyke a bold out-law,
    And robbed all the north country.

The king he writt an a letter then,
    A letter which was large and long;
He signed it with his owner hand;
    And he promised to doe him no wrong.

When this letter came Johnie untill,   (*unto*)
    His heart it was as blythe as birds on the tree:
"Never was I sent for before any king,
    My father, my grandfather, nor none but mee.

"And if wee goe the king before,
    I would we went most orderly;
Every man of you shall have his scarlet cloak,
    Lacèd with silver laces three.

"Every won of you shall have his velvett coat,
    Laced with silver lace so white;
O the golden bands an about your necks,
    Black hatts, white feathers, all alyke."

By the morrow morninge at ten of the clock,
    Towards Edenburough gon was hee,
And with him all his eight score men;
    Good Lord, it was a goodly sight for to see!

When Johnie came befower the king,
    He fell downe on his knee;
"O pardon, my soveraine leige," he said,
    "O pardon my eight score men and mee!"

"Thou shalt have no pardon, thou traytor strong,
    For thy eight score men nor thee;
For tomorrow morning by ten of the clock,
    Both thou and them shall hang on the gallow-tree."

But Johnie looke'd over his left shoulder,
    Good Lord, what a grievous look looked hee!
Saying, "Asking grace of a graceles face —
    Why there is none for you nor me."

But Johnie had a bright sword by his side,
    And it was made of the mettle so free,
That had not the king stept his foot aside,
    He had smitten his head from his faire bodde.

Saying, "Fight on, my merry men all,
    And see that none of you be taine;
For rather then men shall say we were hange'd,
    Let them report how we were slaine."

Then, God wott, faire Eddenburrough rose,
    And so besett poore Johnie rounde,
That fowerscore and tenn of Johnie's best men
    Lay gasping all upon the ground.

Then like a mad man Johnie laid about,
   And like a mad man then fought hee,
Untill a falce Scot came Johnie behinde,
   And runn him through the faire boddee.

Saying, "Fight on, my merry men all,
   And see that none of you be taine;
For I will stand by and bleed but awhile,
   And then will I come and fight againe."

Newes then was brought to young Johnie Armstrong,
   As he stood by his nurse's knee,
Who vowed if ere he live'd for to be a man,
   On the treacherous Scots revenged hee'd be.

—SCOTTISH BALLAD

Do you think the young Johnie Armstrong (mentioned in the last stanza) had good reason to vow revenge?

Why did the king write to Johnie? What comparison tells you how Johnie felt about receiving the letter? What do Johnie's reaction and his preparations suggest about his character?

What is your opinion of the king? Why did Johnie fight? What do you think happened after Johnie died?

Why do you think Johnie was such a hero in his own time that someone wrote a song about him? Why do you suppose this ballad is still popular today?

► ► ►

Who are the heroes of the American past? Why do we admire them?

THE STREETS OF LAREDO

As I walked out in the streets of Laredo,
As I walked out in Laredo one day,
I spied a young cowboy all wrapped in white linen,
All wrapped in white linen as cold as the clay.

"I see by your outfit that you are a cowboy" —
These words he did say as I boldly stepped by,
"Come sit down beside me and hear my sad story;
I'm shot in the breast and I know I must die.

"It was once in the saddle I used to go dashing,
Once in the saddle I used to go gay;
First to the ale-house and then to the jail-house,
Got shot in the breast and I'm dying today.

"Get six jolly cowboys to carry my coffin;
Get six pretty maidens to carry my pall;
Put bunches of roses all over my coffin,
Roses to deaden the clods as they fall.

"Oh, beat the drum slowly and play the fife lowly,
Play the dead march as you carry me along;
Take me to the green valley and lay the sod o'er me,
For I'm a young cowboy and I know I've done wrong.

"Go gather around you a crowd of young cowboys
And tell them the story of this, my sad fate;
Tell one and the other before they go further
To stop their wild roving before it's too late.

"Go fetch me a cup, a cup of cold water
To cool my parched lips," the cowboy then said.
Before I returned, the spirit had left him
And gone to its Maker—the cowboy was dead.

We beat the drum slowly and played the fife lowly,
And bitterly wept as we carried him along;
For we all loved our comrade, so brave, young, and hand-
    some,
We all loved our comrade although he'd done wrong.

—AMERICAN BALLAD

Why do you think the cowboys had all loved their comrade?
Do you think the cowboy had harmed other people?

If you were singing this song, which lines in the first four
stanzas should be relatively lively? Which should be slow? How
should the rest of the song sound?

This ballad is probably an American version of a much older
English song. How is the dying cowboy's story a typical Ameri-
can story? How is it a story that might have happened at any
time, in any place?

▶ ▶ ▶

Harriet Tubman is a famous ex-slave who, before the Civil War, led uncounted numbers of slaves out of the South to freedom in the North via the Underground Railroad.

HARRIET TUBMAN

Dark is the face of Harriet,
Darker still her fate
Deep in the dark of southern wilds
Deep in the slavers' hate.

Fiery the eye of Harriet,
Fiery, dark, and wild;
Bitter, bleak, and hopeless
Is the bonded child.

Stand in the fields, Harriet,
Stand alone and still
Stand before the overseer
Mad enough to kill.

This is slavery, Harriet,
Bend beneath the lash;
This is Maryland, Harriet,
Bow to poor white trash.

You're a field hand, Harriet,
Working the corn;
You're a grubber with the hoe
And a slave child born.

You're just sixteen, Harriet,
And never had a beau;
Your mother's dead long time ago,
Your daddy you don't know.

This piece of iron's not hard enough
To kill you with a blow,
This piece of iron can't hurt you,
Just let you slaves all know.

I'm still the overseer,
Old marster'll believe my tale;
I know that he will keep me,
From going to the jail.

Get up, bleeding Harriet,
I didn't hit you hard;
Get up, bleeding Harriet,
And grease your head with lard.

Get up, sullen Harriet,
Get up and bind your head.
Remember this is Maryland
And I can beat you dead.

How far is the road to Canada?
How far do I have to go?
How far is the road from Maryland
And the hatred that I know?

I stabbed that overseer;
I took his rusty knife;
I killed that overseer;
I took his lowdown life.

For three long years I waited,
Three years I kept my hate,
Three years before I killed him,
Three years I had to wait.

Done shook the dust of Maryland
Clean off my weary feet;
I'm on my way to Canada
And Freedom's golden street.

I'm bound to git to Canada
Before another week;
I come through swamps and mountains,
I waded many a creek.

Now tell my brothers yonder
That Harriet is free;
Yes, tell my brothers yonder
No more auction block for me.

· · · ·

Come down from the mountain, Harriet,
Come down to the valley at night,
Come down to your weeping people
And be their guiding light.

Sing Deep Dark River of Jordan,
Don't you want to cross over today?
Sing Deep Wide River of Jordan,
Don't you want to walk Freedom's way?

I stole down in the night time,
I come back in the day,
I stole back to my Maryland
To guide the slaves away.

I met old marster yonder
A-coming down the road,
And right past me in Maryland
My old marster strode.

I passed beside my marster
And covered up my head;
My marster didn't know me
I guess he heard I'm dead.

I wonder if he thought about
That overseer's dead;
I wonder if he figured out
He ought to know this head?

You better run, brave Harriet,
There's ransom on your head;
You better run, Miss Harriet,
They want you live or dead.

Been down in valleys yonder
And searching round the stills,
They got the posse after you,
A-riding through the hills.

They got the blood hounds smelling,
They got their guns cocked too;
You better run, bold Harriet,
The white man's after you.

They got ten thousand dollars
Put on your coal-black head;
They'll give ten thousand dollars;
They're mad because you fled.

I wager they'll be riding
A long, long time for you.
Yes, Lord, they'll look a long time
Till Judgment Day is due.

. . . .

I'm Harriet Tubman, people,
I'm Harriet, the slave,
I'm Harriet, free woman,
And I'm free within my grave.

> *Come along, children, with Harriet*
> *Come along, children, come along*
> *Uncle Sam is rich enough*
> *To give you all a farm.*

I killed the overseer.
I fooled old marster's eyes,
I found my way to Canada
With hundreds more besides.

> *Come along to Harper's Ferry*
> *Come along to brave John Brown*
> *Come along with Harriet, children,*
> *Come along ten million strong.*

I met the mighty John Brown,
I know Fred Douglass too
Enlisted Abolitionists
Beneath the Union blue.

I heard the mighty trumpet
That sent the land to war;
I mourned for Mister Lincoln
And saw his funeral car.

Come along with Harriet, children,
Come along to Canada.
Come down to the river, children,
And follow the northern star.

I'm Harriet Tubman, People,
I'm Harriet, the slave,
I'm Harriet, free woman,
And I'm free beyond my grave.

Come along to freedom, children,
Come along ten million strong;
Come along with Harriet, children,
Come along ten million strong.

—MARGARET WALKER

Stories of Experiences

When you like someone very much, how does your feeling change the way you do everything?

> Oh, when I was in love with you,
>   Then I was clean and brave,
> And miles around the wonder grew
>   How well did I behave.
>
> And now the fancy passes by,
>   And nothing will remain,
> And miles around they'll say that I
>   Am quite myself again.

—A. E. HOUSMAN

► ► ►

When might you enjoy being out in falling snow?

DRIVING TO TOWN LATE TO MAIL A LETTER

> It is a cold and snowy night. The main street is
>   deserted.
> The only things moving are swirls of snow.
> As I lift the mailbox door, I feel its cold iron.
> There is a privacy I love in this snowy night.
> Driving around, I will waste more time.

—ROBERT BLY

Judging from the reason for coming and from the look of the main street, do you visualize a large or small town? What does the poet feel physically? What does he feel emotionally? How does he plan to express that emotion?

INCIDENT

for Eric Walrond

Once riding in old Baltimore,
    Heart-filled, head-filled with glee,
I saw a Baltimorean
    Keep looking straight at me.

Now I was eight and very small,
    And he was no whit bigger,
And so I smiled, but he poked out
    His tongue, and called me, 'Nigger'.

I saw the whole of Baltimore
    From May until December;
Of all the things that happened there
    That's all that I remember.

                —COUNTEE CULLEN

Eric Walrond, to whom this poem is dedicated, is a black poet, like Countee Cullen.

Why do you think people call other people names? What is the effect on you of being called a name you don't like?

97

What is your favorite game? Why do you like to play it?

DUCK-CHASING

I spied a very small brown duck
Riding the swells of the sea
Like a rocking-chair. "Little duck!"
I cried. It paddled away,
I paddled after it. When it dived,
Down I dived: too smoky was the sea,
We were lost. It surfaced
In the west, I torpedoed west
And when it dived I dived,
And we were lost and lost and lost
In the slant smoke of the sea.
When I came floating up on it
From the side, like a deadman,
And yelled suddenly, it took off,
It skimmed the swells as it ascended,
Brown wings burning and flashing
In the sun as the sea it rose over
Burned and flashed underneath it.
I did not see the little duck again.
Duck-chasing is a game like any game.
When it is over it is all over.

—GALWAY KINNELL

What is the fun of playing duck-chasing?

Could you write out the rules for duck-chasing from the story this poem tells? How does the game begin? After it starts, what are the next moves? Do you think the game is played exactly the same way each time?

How do you think the player would feel if he really did catch the duck?

Notice the verbs in the poem. Suppose instead of *spied*, the first line had said *saw*. How would the meaning be different? For any other verb in the poem, can you suggest another way to say what either the duck or the player did? For instance, how else could you say that the duck *surfaced*? What happens when you try to change a verb?

Why do you think the poet repeated *lost* three times in one line? What initial letter is repeated most frequently in this poem? How does that sound suit the setting?

What other activities might you consider games? How is a game all over after you have played it? What about it might last? How does this poem make the game of duck-chasing last?

Why do deer sometimes stand very still? How might you become aware of their presence?

THE BUCK IN THE SNOW

White sky, over the hemlocks bowed with snow,
Saw you not at the beginning of evening the antlered buck
    and his doe
Standing in the apple-orchard? I saw them. I saw them
    suddenly go,
Tails up, with long leaps lovely and slow,
Over the stone-wall into the wood of hemlocks bowed
    with snow.

Now lies he here, his wild blood scalding the snow.

How strange a thing is death, bringing to his knees,
    bringing to his antlers
The buck in the snow.
How strange a thing,—a mile away by now, it may be,
Under the heavy hemlocks that as the moments pass
Shift their loads a little, letting fall a feather of snow—
Life, looking out attentive from the eyes of the doe.

—EDNA ST. VINCENT MILLAY

How does the poet seem to feel about the death of the buck? Why do you think she feels that way?

If you were illustrating this poem, which medium would you use: pencil, ink, charcoal, pastels, tempera, watercolors, or oils? Why?

What is the effect of having the second stanza only one line long?

How does the sound of the main rhyme fit the way the deer move? What repeated patterns of initial letters connect words?

Compare the rhyme of the first six lines to the rhyme of the last six. How does the difference fit the experience the poem tells?

Suppose that one night you found a deer dead on a curve of a winding mountain road. What would you do?

TRAVELING THROUGH THE DARK

Traveling through the dark I found a deer
dead on the edge of the Wilson River road.
It is usually best to roll them into the canyon:
that road is narrow; to swerve might make more dead.

By glow of the tail-light I stumbled back of the car
and stood by the heap, a doe, a recent killing;
she had stiffened already, almost cold.
I dragged her off; she was large in the belly.

My fingers touching her side brought me the reason —
her side was warm; her fawn lay there waiting,
alive, still, never to be born.
Beside that mountain road I hesitated.

The car aimed ahead its lowered parking lights;
under the hood purred the steady engine.
I stood in the glare of the warm exhaust turning red;
around our group I could hear the wilderness listen.

I thought hard for us all — my only swerving —,
then pushed her over the edge into the river.

—WILLIAM STAFFORD

What did the speaker do with the deer? What kept him from doing it immediately? Why do you think he finally did it?

What are the sources of the two kinds of warmth in the poem? In what ways are they different? What word imitates the sound of one of the sources?

What kind of noises would a listening wilderness make? What might it be listening for?

What kind of swerving does the first stanza talk about? How can one person think for others ("my only swerving"): by doing the thinking for them without giving them a chance to think for themselves, OR by thinking about their safety? Why didn't he consult the others in the car?

Do you think the experience would have ended differently if it had happened during the day? What other kinds of dark are there besides the dark at night? How do people travel through other kinds of darkness? Do they always know the right thing to do?

► ► ►

As we got
Closer, the
Rainbow disappeared.

—JULIUS LESTER

By what signs can you tell that a storm is coming?

What hardships can happen to a horse in its lifetime? Do horses give up easily?

SILVER

I thought Silver must have snaked logs
      when young:
she couldn't stand to have the line brush her lower hind leg:
in blinded halter she couldn't tell what had loosened behind her
         and was coming
as downhill
to rush into her crippling her to the ground:
and when she almost went to sleep, me dreaming at the slow plow,
I would
at dream's end turning over the mind to a new chapter
      let the line drop and touch her leg
      and she would
bring the plow out of the ground with speed but wisely
fall soon again into the slow requirements of our dreams:
how we turned at the ends of rows without sense to new furrows
and went back
        flicked by
      cornblades and hearing the circling in
the cornblades of horseflies in pursuit:

I hitch up early, the raw spot on Silver's shoulder
sore to the collar,
get a wrench and change the plow's bull-tongue for a sweep,
and go out, wrench in my hip pocket for later adjustments,
        down the ditch-path
by the white-bloomed briars, wet crabgrass, cattails,
                and rusting ferns,
riding the plow handles down,

keeping the sweep's point from the ground,
the smooth bar under the plow gliding,
the traces loose, the raw spot wearing its soreness out
in the gentle movement to the fields:

            when snake-bitten in the spring pasture grass
Silver came up to the gate and stood head-down enchanted
            in her fate
I found her sorrowful eyes by accident and knew:
nevertheless the doctor could not keep her from all
the consequences, rolls in the sand, the blank extension
            of limbs,
            head thrown back in the dust,
useless unfocusing eyes, belly swollen
wide as I was tall
and I went out in the night and saw her in the solitude
            of her wildness:

but she lived and one day half got up
and looking round at the sober world took me back
            into her eyes
and then got up and walked and plowed again;
mornings her swollen snake-bitten leg wept bright as dew
and dried to streaks of salt leaked white from the hair.

                                        —A. R. AMMONS

Do you admire Silver? Why? The poet has said that the real Silver was a mule. Is there anything in the poem that gives you a clue about whether she is a mule or a horse? Does it make any difference to you?

How old do you think the "I" of this poem was when he plowed with Silver? What different things did he notice about the cornfields and the ditch-path? How does his noticing tell you the way he feels about his work? What other clues to his feeling do you find?

How was he able to save Silver's life? What couldn't he save her from? Why do you think he went out to visit her, even though he couldn't really help her?

Why do you think the narrator compares the discharge from Silver's wound to the brightness of dew? Is dew a part of nature? Were Silver's snake-bite and her recovery a part of nature? Why do you think the narrator plowed with Silver before the wound was completely healed?

Have you ever tried to catch a firefly? Why try?

The first firefly . . .
But he got away
And I . . .
Air in my fingers.

—ISSA

How would it feel to catch air rather than a firefly? Do you think the experience made the poet unhappy?

▶ ▶ ▶

5
Poems
Describe

When you try to tell someone else about an experience, you are likely to talk about what it was *like*. "It tasted like soap," you might say after taking a bite of stale cheese cake. The comparison tells your listener at once how unpleasant the taste was.

Often, also, when you want to describe something, you compare it to something else. A clothing advertisement might refer to a "charcoal jacket," for instance. No one is going to think that the jacket is made of charcoal or necessarily feels like a piece of charcoal. What will the comparison tell readers about the jacket?

A comparison can help you recognize something familiar in the unfamiliar. That way you can begin to understand. Everyday talk is full of comparisons. For instance, you might describe a classmate's eating habits by saying, "She eats like a bird." What other common expressions like these can you think of?

But does a girl who takes tiny bites very quickly eat the same food that a bird eats? No; whenever you compare one thing to something else, there are always differences.

Sometimes, instead of comparing, a poem will contrast. A contrast emphasizes the differences between things rather than the similarities. It puts two very different things next to each other for a purpose. White next to black looks whiter than it does next to grey.

Yet, though white and black *are* different, they *do* have something in common. They are both colors. If two things are completely different, you really can't contrast them easily. You'd hardly ever think of them together. For instance, can you think of a way to contrast the color red to the shape of an egg?

Can you think of two things that contrast especially sharply for you? What do they have in common? Can you think of two things that are so completely different you can't contrast them?

The most complete way to tell an experience or to describe something is to picture it in detail. A picturing poem may use either comparisons or contrasts, or it may use both. It often reminds you that things are *both* alike and different. Every experience, every person, every thing has something in common with something else in the world. At the same time, every experience, every person, every thing is unique. There is nothing else in the world exactly like it.

Poems Describe by Comparing

The Pueblo Indians depended on rain for their crops. To encourage the rain to come, they used to chant rain songs.

SONG OF THE SKY LOOM

O our Mother the Earth, O our Father the Sky,
Your children are we, and with tired backs
We bring you the gifts that you love.
Then weave for us a garment of brightness;
May the warp be the white light of morning,
May the weft be the red light of evening,
May the fringes be the falling rain,
May the border be the standing rainbow.
Thus weave for us a garment of brightness
That we may walk fittingly where birds sing,
That we may walk fittingly where grass is green,
O our Mother the Earth, O our Father the Sky!

—AMERICAN INDIAN CHANT

What does this song call the earth, the sky, and the people? What do the names suggest earth, sky, and people are all a part of?

The warp on a loom is the lengthwise series of parallel threads. These threads are more tightly twisted and are put on the loom first. Then the weaver gradually fills in the weft threads, which extend from side to side. What are to be the warp and the weft of the garment in the poem? Why do you suppose each was chosen for its particular part, rather than the other way around?

How will this garment be trimmed? Why would the Indians think of those parts of the sky as trimming?

What reason does the song give for the Indians' request? What seems to be the Indians' relationship to nature?

► ► ►

SENSE OF SOMETHING COMING

I am like a flag in the center of open space.
I sense ahead the wind which is coming, and must
    live it through,
While the creatures of the world beneath still do not
    move in their sleep:
The doors still close softly, and the chimneys are
    full of silence,
The windows do not rattle yet, and the dust still
    lies down.

I already know the storm, and I am as troubled as
    the sea,
And spread myself out, and fall into myself,
And throw myself out and am absolutely alone
In the great storm.

—RAINER MARIA RILKE
(translated by Robert Bly)

In an approaching storm, how is a flag's climate different from the climate on the ground? What happens to a person who feels a sense of something coming?

The flag, of course, reacts to the weather. What do people react to? What other kinds of approaching storms might one person be aware of, while everyone else goes about business as usual?

111

How do most modern people feel about the way time passes in a day?

The clock
on the bookcase ticks,
the watch on the table ticks—
these busy insects
are eating away my world.

—CHARLES REZNIKOFF

What does the comparison tell you about the speaker's feelings about time?

► ► ►

Have you ever seen a face that vaguely reminded you of something? Were you ever able to say what it reminded you of?

Someone, somewhere—there's
Something about that face . . .
That's it—the viper!

—ISSA

► ► ►

How do you feel when someone you like goes away for a while?

SEPARATION

Your absence has gone through me
Like thread through a needle.
Everything I do is stitched with its color.

—W. S. MERWIN

What color would you choose to express the feeling of absence? How might the feeling affect what you do?

▶ ▶ ▶

from KARINTHA

Her skin is like dusk on the eastern horizon,
O cant you see it, O cant you see it,
Her skin is like dusk on the eastern horizon
... When the sun goes down.

—JEAN TOOMER

How would it feel to be famous?

Fame is a bee.
    It has a song—
It has a sting—
    Ah, too, it has a wing.

—EMILY DICKINSON

In what ways does the poem say fame and a bee are alike? What does each way suggest about how a famous person feels? Does the poem as a whole make you wish to be famous?

▶ ▶ ▶

How does a window-dresser move as he arranges a display,
say in a crowded window of a china-store?

Spring is like a perhaps hand
(which comes carefully
out of Nowhere) arranging
a window, into which people look (while
people stare
arranging and changing placing
carefully there a strange
thing and a known thing here) and

changing everything carefully

spring is like a perhaps
Hand in a window
(carefully to
and fro moving New and
Old things, while
people stare carefully
moving a perhaps
fraction of flower here placing
an inch of air there) and

without breaking anything.

— E. E. CUMMINGS

How is Spring like a hand reaching through the back of a
store window to arrange it? What other kind of store window,
besides a china-store window, might need to be arranged in a
similar way?

What would be "perhaps" about a window-dresser's hand?
Why does a window dresser sometimes put things, first one

place, then another? When Spring first appears, are you ever completely sure that it's here to stay?

How long does it take Spring to arrive? How long does it take a window-dresser to arrange a complete display?

What word is repeated most often? How often? Why do you think the poet repeats that word more often than any other? How is that word moved around in the poem? What other repeated words are moved around in a similar way?

How is the first line of the second stanza different from the first line of the first stanza? How does the new arrangement fit the idea of the whole poem?

► ► ►

CITY: SAN FRANCISCO

In the morning the city
Spreads its wings
Making a song
In stone that sings.

In the evening the city
Goes to bed
Hanging lights
About its head.

—LANGSTON HUGHES

What does the city seem to be like in the morning? What does it seem to be like in the evening? Are the two comparisons appropriate for a city in ways other than those Langston Hughes mentions?

What things or experiences might a lonely place remind you of?

VACANCY IN THE PARK

March . . . Someone has walked across the
    snow,
Someone looking for he knows not what.

It is like a boat that has pulled away
From a shore at night and disappeared.

It is like a guitar left on a table
By a woman, who has forgotten it.

It is like the feeling of a man
Come back to see a certain house.

The four winds blow through the rustic arbor,
Under its mattresses of vines.

—WALLACE STEVENS

What is the vacancy in the park like? Is the park an attractive place?

March snow is often thin and soft, easily melted. How would footprints show up in such snow? What would make them appear aimless? How might such footprints be like March weather?

Why would a boat pull away from a shore? Would it necessarily make any noise?

Would a forgotten guitar be making music? What sound does the March in this poem make?

How might it feel to come back to see a house you had lived in long ago? What details in the poem give you clues about the condition of the house? How is its condition like the condition of the park?

In March, what is the park vacant of?

► ► ►

HALF MOON

The moon goes over the water.
How tranquil the sky is!
She goes scything slowly
the old shimmer from the river;
meanwhile a young frog
takes her for a little mirror.

—FEDERICO GARCIA LORCA
(translated by W. S. Merwin)

What does the moon seem to be doing to the river? How would a young frog act to show that he thinks the reflected moon is a mirror?

If you have never been in a subway station, can you imagine what one looks like?

Walk about the subway station
in a grove of steel pillars;
how their knobs, the rivet-heads —
unlike those of oaks —
are regularly placed;
how barren the ground is
except here and there on the platform
a flat black fungus
that was chewing-gum.

—CHARLES REZNIKOFF

What do the pillars of the subway station remind the poet of? How are the pillars different? What else in the station fits in with the comparison?

Does the main comparison make the subway station seem pleasant or unpleasant?

► ► ►

What do you think it would be like to be without a body and still be yourself? What would you miss being able to do?

QUESTION

Body my house
my horse my hound
what will I do
when you are fallen

Where will I sleep
How will I ride
What will I hunt

Where can I go
without my mount
all eager and quick
How will I know
in thicket ahead
is danger or treasure
when Body my good
bright dog is dead

How will it be
to lie in the sky
without roof or door
and wind for an eye

With cloud for shift
how will I hide?

—MAY SWENSON

► ► ►

Poems Describe by Contrasting

Imagine a butterfly asleep on a large bell. How would the butterfly be different from the bell in size and shape? How would they feel different if you touched them?

> Butterfly asleep
>> Folded soft on
>> Temple bell . . .
> Then bronze gong rang!

—BUSON

What do you imagine happened when the bronze gong rang? How would the butterfly contrast with the bell then?

▶ ▶ ▶

Have you ever seen flowers growing in surprising places?

> Now in late Autumn
>> Look, on my old
>> Rubbish-heap . . .
> Blue morning-glory

—TAIGI

Think of two entirely different sounds. What do they have in common?

THE VOICE THAT BEAUTIFIES THE LAND

1

The voice that beautifies the land!
The voice above,
The voice of the thunder,
Among the dark clouds
Again and again it sounds,
The voice that beautifies the land.

2

The voice that beautifies the land!
The voice below,
The voice of the grasshopper,
Among the flowers and grasses
Again and again it sounds,
The voice that beautifies the land.

—AMERICAN INDIAN CHANT

Among all the other sounds of nature, why do you suppose the Navaho Indians chose these two voices for their chant?

► ► ►

Have you ever seen a very old mirror? Was there anything special about it?

THE MIRROR IN THE WOODS

A mirror hung on the broken
Walls of an old summer house
Deep in the dark woods. Nothing
Ever moved in it but the
Undersea shadows of ferns,
Rhododendrons and redwoods.
Moss covered the frame. One day
The gold and glue gave way and
The mirror slipped to the floor.
For many more years it stood
On the shattered boards. Once in
A long time a wood rat would
Pass it by without ever

Looking in. At last we came,
Breaking the sagging door and
Letting in a narrow wedge
Of sunlight. We took the mirror
Away and hung it in my
Daughter's room with a barre before
It. Now it reflects ronds, escartes,
Relevés and arabesques.
In the old house the shadows,
The wood rats and moss work unseen.

—KENNETH REXROTH

What is unusual about finding a mirror deep in the woods?
What kind of movements would ferns, rhododendrons, and
redwoods make? What would make their reflections look as if
they were undersea? Why do you think the poet calls their
reflections "shadows"?

How useful was the mirror on the floor of the cabin?

A *barre* is a fixed rod a ballerina grasps while she practices.
Ronds, *escartes*, *relevés*, and *arabesques* are ballet movements.
How does what the mirror reflects in the girl's room contrast
with what it reflected in the woods? Would the movements of
the plants and of the dancer look alike in any way? Why would
a dancer need a mirror?

► ► ►

An incantation is a magic chant.

INCANTATION

A white well
In a black cave;
A bright shell
In a dark wave.

A white rose
Black brambles hood;
Smooth bright snows
In a dark wood.

A flung white glove
In a dark fight;
A white dove
On a wild black night.

A white door
In a dark lane;
A bright core
To bitter black pain.

A white hand
Waved from dark walls;
In a burnt black land
Bright waterfalls.

—ELINOR WYLIE

If you were painting a picture or making a design to fit this poem, what color would you use most? How large, proportionately, would each bit of contrast actually be? How important would it seem to be? Why?

124

What word does the poet use alternately for black and for white? What other adjectives does the poet also use for each color? What feelings do the alternate words and additional adjectives express?

A white glove flung down in the middle of a fight would be a sign of surrender. If you were wandering, frightened, down a dark, walled street, what might it mean to see a white door suddenly?

Sometimes, when you are hurt, you see everything around you more clearly than you ever have before. What extra meaning would brightness have, if it came out of pain? What deeper meaning might each of the other white things in the poem have, if you found them in blackness?

What color does the poem begin with? What color does it end with? What magic does this poem hope to bring about? Do you think the magic is possible?

► ► ►

Where do live lambs belong? Where do dead lambs belong?

FOR A LAMB

I saw on the slant hill a putrid lamb,
Propped with daisies. The sleep looked deep,
The face nudged in the green pillow
But the guts were out for crows to eat.
Where's the lamb? whose tender plaint
Said all for the mute breezes.
Say he's in the wind somewhere,
Say, there's a lamb in the daisies.

—RICHARD EBERHART

► ► ►

125

The centaur is a mythological creature with the head of a man and the body of a horse. The legendary unicorn had the body and head of a horse, the hind legs of a stag, the tail of a lion, and, in the middle of his forehead, a single, long, straight corkscrew horn.

What are you doing in our street among the automobiles, horse?
How are your cousins, the centaur and the unicorn?

—CHARLES REZNIKOFF

How has the horse become similar to the centaur and the unicorn? How is he different? What else in the poem does he contrast with?

► ► ►

Poems Describe by Picturing

What does an orchard in bloom look like?

Loveliest of trees, the cherry now
Is hung with bloom along the bough,
And stands about the woodland ride
Wearing white for Eastertide.

Now, of my threescore years and ten,
Twenty will not come again,
And take from seventy springs a score,
It only leaves me fifty more.

And since to look at things in bloom
Fifty springs are little room,
About the woodlands I will go
To see the cherry hung with snow.

—A. E. HOUSMAN

Why does the speaker want to go to see the cherry trees?

How long is the average lifetime for a human being? How many years of life does the speaker have left? What would he do if he had more time?

In some climates, snow can come even while fruit trees are blooming. Are the cherry trees in this poem hung with real snow?

The sloth lives in Central and South America. If you are lucky, you may have seen one in a zoo. The sloth's name comes from the old English word for *slow*.

THE SLOTH

In moving-slow he has no Peer.
You ask him something in his ear;
He thinks about it for a Year;

And, then, before he says a Word
There, upside down (unlike a Bird)
He will assume that you have Heard —

A most Ex-as-per-at-ing Lug.
But should you call his manner Smug,
He'll sigh and give his Branch a Hug;

Then off again to Sleep he goes,
Still swaying gently by his Toes,
And you just *know* he knows he knows.

—THEODORE ROETHKE

Would you like to try to have a conversation with a sloth?

How does the sloth answer questions? How courteously does he treat his questioners?

Do people sometimes move and act like the sloth? If they do, do you like it?

Does a bird seem to be as comfortable on the ground as he is in the air?

"A BIRD CAME DOWN THE WALK"

A Bird came down the Walk—
He did not know I saw—
He bit an Angleworm in halves
And ate the fellow, raw,

And then he drank a Dew
From a convenient Grass—
And then hopped sidewise to the Wall
To let a Beetle pass—

He glanced with rapid eyes
That hurried all around—
They looked like frightened Beads, I thought—
He stirred his Velvet Head

Like one in danger, Cautious,
I offered him a Crumb
And he unrolled his feathers
And rowed him softer home—

Than Oars divide the Ocean,
Too silver for a seam—
Or Butterflies, off Banks of Noon
Leap, splashless as they swim.

—EMILY DICKINSON

Where is this bird more at home? Why is he on the ground? Would you like to see him eat the angleworm?

Why does he fly away? What did his flight look like? What kind of ocean wouldn't show even the slightest seam?

129

Picture in your mind an animal who isn't moving. What might he be doing?

& sun &
sil
e
nce
e

very

w
here
noon
e

is exc

ep
t
on
t

his

b
oul
der
a

drea(chipmunk)ming

—E. E. CUMMINGS

▶ ▶ ▶

At a distance from a meadow, is it easy to distinguish grazing sheep from boulders?

THE KILL

Sheep move on the grass
so little one imagines
small boulders.

Then a dog hurtles
into the field, like water.

The sheep flutter.
The dog tears among them
for five minutes. Then he diminishes

like a wind or a flood
into the rubble of distance.

—DONALD HALL

Why don't the sheep move very much?

When might water be said to *hurtle*? What does comparing the way the dog moves to water hurtling suggest about the way the dog disturbs the sheep?

What kind of living things usually flutter? What do the sheep seem to be like?

What causes the wind to blow or water to flood? What causes the dog to attack the sheep, and then run away?

Rubble is loose, rough, fragmented stone. It may come from a quarry or from the decay or destruction of a building. Does rubble here describe the field itself, or what the dog leaves behind him, or both?

How do you know what has happened in the field? Why do you think the poet doesn't picture the kill itself?

► ► ►

Catching fish is only a part of a fisherman's work. The fish must also be cleaned and prepared for market.

FISHING HARBOUR TOWARDS EVENING

Slashed clouds leak gold. Along the slurping wharf
The snugged boats creak and seesaw. Round the masts

Abrasive squalls flake seagulls off the sky:
Choppy with wings the rapids of shrill sound.

Wrapt in spliced airs of fish and tar,
Light wincing on their knives, the clockwork men

Incise and scoop the oily pouches, flip
The soft guts overboard with blood-wet fingers.

Among three rhythms the slapping silver turns
To polished icy marble upon the deck.

—RICHARD KELL

What is happening on this evening?

This poet has used words in unusual ways to picture the sights, sounds, and smells of the fishing harbor and the physical sensations of the fishermen. What kind of clouds would be "slashed" so that they would seem to "leak gold"? How can a wharf be "slurping"? What makes the boats "creak" and "seesaw"?

What does saying that the squalls "*flake* seagulls off the sky" suggest the seagulls look like? What do the gulls sound like?

What do the boats smell of? How are the men working? Why do they work that way? How do their hands feel?

What movement has caused each of the three rhythms mentioned in the last stanza? What one word from each of the first three stanzas fits each rhythm most closely?

What sound do the fish make as the men work on them? What becomes of the fish?

► ► ►

With its fog-shroud the
Bridge looks like the Gate to Heaven.
The water is deep.

—JULIUS LESTER

133

Think of someone you admire very much, but don't know very well. Why do you admire him? Do you think he is happy?

RICHARD CORY

Whenever Richard Cory went down town,
We people on the pavement looked at him:
He was a gentleman from sole to crown,
Clean favored, and imperially slim.

And he was always quietly arrayed,
And he was always human when he talked;
But still he fluttered pulses when he said,
"Good-morning," and he glittered when he walked.

And he was rich—yes, richer than a king—
And admirably schooled in every grace:
In fine, we thought that he was everything
To make us wish that we were in his place.

So on we worked, and waited for the light,
And went without the meat, and cursed the bread;
And Richard Cory, one calm summer night,
Went home and put a bullet through his head.

—EDWIN ARLINGTON ROBINSON

How does this poem picture Richard Cory's appearance? How did he usually act?

How rich is he? What other words in the poem fit with this comparison?

What were the townspeople like? Do you think they understood Richard Cory?

► ► ►

What does a house show about the person who lives in it?

JERÓNIMO'S HOUSE

My house, my fairy
    palace, is
of perishable
    clapboards with
three rooms in all,
    my gray wasps' nest
of chewed-up paper
    glued with spit.

My home, my love-nest
    is endowed
with a veranda
    of wooden lace,
adorned with ferns
    planted in sponges,
and the front room
    with red and green

left-over Christmas
    decorations
looped from the corners
    to the middle
above my little
    center table
of woven wicker
    painted blue,

and four blue chairs
    and an affair
for the smallest baby
    with a tray
with ten big beads.
    Then on the walls
two palm-leaf fans
    and a calendar

and on the table
    one fried fish
spattered with burning
    scarlet sauce,
a little dish
    of hominy grits
and four pink tissue-
    paper roses.

Also I have
    hung on a hook,
an old French horn
    repainted with
aluminum paint.
    I play each year
in the parade
    for José Marti.

At night you'd think
my house abandoned.
Come closer. You
can see and hear
the writing-paper
lines of light
and the voices of
my radio

singing flamencos
in between
the lottery numbers.
When I move
I take these things,
not much more, from
my shelter from
the hurricane.

—ELIZABETH BISHOP

What kind of person does Jerónimo seem to be? In what
climate do you think he lives?

What is Jerónimo's house built of? A wasp builds its celled
nest by chewing wood fiber. When Jerónimo calls his house a
gray wasps' nest, what does he suggest about how strongly the
house was built? Who probably built it?

How does the veranda resemble the ferns? Do you think
Jerónimo is proud of his house? What words give you clues to
his feeling?

What do the colors inside the house tell you about Jerónimo?

How many chairs are there? How many beads on the baby's
chair? How many fans? What other things does he count? Why
do you think he counts so carefully?

What do you have to do at night to discover that someone
lives in Jerónimo's house? Why do you think the poet has
Jerónimo tell you about his house in his own words?

How strong a shelter from the hurricane do you think Jer-
ónimo's house really is? Considering everything he tells you
about his house, do you think he is happy?

► ► ►

How would you picture the movements of spring?

SPRING IMAGES

Two athletes
Are dancing in the cathedral
Of the wind.

A butterfly lights on the branch
Of your green voice.

Small antelopes
Fall asleep in the ashes
Of the moon.

—JAMES WRIGHT

How does it feel to be running against the wind in the spring? What in nature might look like a cathedral? Why do people build cathedrals? In springtime, might people run for a similar reason?

How does a butterfly light on a branch? Why do we say he *lights*, rather than *settles* or *lands*? How would a green voice sound, as compared to a voice of a different color? What kind of noises does Spring make?

What is Spring like when it sleeps? What color would the ashes of the moon have?

Which of these three images picturing Spring do you like best?

► ► ►

6

Sounds
Shape Poems

When you walk, your footsteps often rise and fall in a somewhat irregular pattern. Sometimes you may stop altogether to look in a store window, and then you wander on. But when might the rhythm of your walk become quite regular? Suppose you start to run; what might happen to the way your feet rise and fall? What would happen then to your heartbeat? Might the rhythm of your running ever become irregular?

A poem, too, is rhythmical. It may have an easy, relaxed, irregular rhythm, like casual walking—or like someone talking. A person talking is sometimes searching for words. He may pause to think. When he's found the right words to express his idea or feeling, he speaks smoothly. Often he repeats. Why do you sometimes repeat something you've said?

Or the rhythm in a poem may be more regular. In a track meet, when a runner hits his stride, his whole body moves in a strong rhythm. In the same way, the words in a poem may rise and fall very regularly when the poet has hit the stride of his thought and feeling.

The rhythm of a poem suggests a mood. Some poems

may sound as slow and serious as a graduation march. Other poems seem almost to dance along. Is the rhythm of your favorite dance irregular, regular, or a combination of both? How does dancing make you feel? How might hearing a poem with a dance-like rhythm make you feel?

The rhythm of a poem also helps to connect the words to each other. Once you've heard the rhythm, it's easier to remember the words of a poem, just as hearing music makes it easier to remember the steps of a dance.

Of course, other patterns of sound besides rhythm connect words and meanings. The most obvious pattern simply repeats words, as in a chorus. Repeated letter sounds create a musical effect too. The repeated sounds can come at the beginning of connected words, or they can come less obviously inside connected words. *Rhyme* makes a special pattern of repeated sound.

Think of a stanza from a poem you remember. Is the rhythm regular, like running in a race, or is it more like strolling along? Does the rhythm imitate something? What mood does it suggest? What other sound patterns do you find?

What is your favorite kind of music? When you hear the music, what mood do you feel?

THE SKY CLEARS

Verily
The sky clears
When my Midé drum
Sounds
For me.
Verily
The waters are smooth
When my Midé drum
Sounds
For me.

—AMERICAN INDIAN SONG

This song comes from the Midé Indians. How does the sound of his drum make the world look to the Indian listener? How do you think he feels when he hears the drum?

Tap out the rhythm of the words of the poem, saying them in your head or aloud. Where do the strong beats come? What does the rhythm of the poem sound like?

What foods do you especially like to eat?

TO A POOR OLD WOMAN

munching a plum on
the street a paper bag
of them in her hand

They taste good to her
They taste good
to her. They taste
good to her

You can see it by
the way she gives herself
to the one half
sucked out in her hand

Comforted
a solace of ripe plums
seeming to fill the air
They taste good to her

—WILLIAM CARLOS WILLIAMS

How does eating the plums seem to make the old woman feel?
Why do you suppose they tasted so good to her?

Who do you think is talking in this poem? Should the repeated
words be read aloud with the same expression? What gives you
a clue about which words to emphasize each time?

► ► ►

How does it feel to be out in the country on a windy spring day?

PLOUGHING ON SUNDAY

The whitecock's tail
Tosses in the wind.
The turkey-cock's tail
Glitters in the sun.

Water in the fields.
The wind pours down.
The feathers flare
And bluster in the wind.

Remus, blow your horn!
I'm ploughing on Sunday,
Ploughing North America.
Blow your horn!

Tum-ti-tum,
Ti-tum-tum-tum!
The turkey-cock's tail
Spreads to the sun.

The whitecock's tail
Streams to the moon.
Water in the fields.
The wind pours down.

—WALLACE STEVENS

Do you think the ploughman is enjoying his work? What makes you think he is or isn't?

What verbs picture the appearance of the whitecock and the turkey-cock? How do the verbs show the kind of day it is?

What kind of wind would *pour* down? Why do you think the poet repeats the lines about the water and the wind?

Why do you think the speaker wants Remus to blow his horn? Who might Remus be? Could anyone plow all of North America on a single Sunday? Why do you think the speaker claims he is?

Say "Tum-ti-tum,/Ti-tum-tum-tum!" aloud. What usually makes the sound pattern it imitates? Where might you hear that sound? What effect does hearing it usually have on you? Does that pattern of sound make the ploughing seem exciting or dull?

When did the man start to plow? When did he stop? What clues suggest his starting and stopping times? How would ploughing on Sunday be different from ploughing on any other day of the week?

▶ ▶ ▶

My horse clip-clopping
 Over a field . . .
 Oh ho!
I'm part of the picture!

—BASHO

In a monologue, one voice speaks without interruption, either to someone else or to himself.

THE SNAIL'S MONOLOGUE

Shall I dwell in my shell?
Shall I not dwell in my shell?
Dwell in shell?
Rather not dwell?
Shall I not dwell,
shall I dwell,
dwell in shell
shall I shell,
shallIshellIshallIshellIshallI . . . ?

(The snail gets so entangled with his thoughts or, rather, the thoughts run away with him so that he must postpone the decision.)

—CHRISTIAN MORGENSTERN
(translated by Max Knight)

With what sounds does the snail's monologue get entangled?

144

On a bright, sunny day, how do waves coming ashore sound?
What sounds do they make on a foggy day?

ALL DAY I HEAR THE NOISE OF WATERS

All day I hear the noise of waters
    Making moan,
Sad as the sea-bird is, when going
    Forth alone,
He hears the winds cry to the waters'
    Monotone.

The grey winds, the cold winds are blowing
    Where I go.
I hear the noise of many waters
    Far below.
All day, all night, I hear them flowing
    To and fro.

—JAMES JOYCE

What kind of weather does this beach have? Would you like
to listen to the noise of these waters?

What lines rhyme? Say only the rhyming words (excluding
waters, which is repeated rather than rhymed). What sound do
the rhyming words imitate, especially when the sound is repeated?

Notice the rhythm of the length of lines. What movement
does the pattern of the lines suggest?

► ► ►

Do you associate lively or dull sounds with winter?

WINTER

from *Love's Labour's Lost*

When icicles hang by the wall,
    And Dick the shepherd blows his nail,
And Tom bears logs into the hall,
    And milk comes frozen home in pail,
When blood is nipped, and ways be foul,
Then nightly sings the staring owl,
      Tu-whit, tu-who!
      A merry note,
While greasy Joan doth keel the pot.

When all around the wind doth blow,
    And coughing drowns the parson's saw,
The birds sit brooding in the snow,
    And Marian's nose looks red and raw,
When roasted crabs hiss in the bowl,
Then nightly sings the staring owl,
      Tu-whit, tu-who!
      A merry note,
While greasy Joan doth keel the pot.

—WILLIAM SHAKESPEARE

What are the "foul" ways of winter in the first stanza? Is there any part of the second stanza that doesn't sound unpleasant? (A *saw* is a wise, but obvious saying, like "Look before you leap." The *crabs* are crab apples baking in a bowl.)

How do people usually think an owl sounds? How does Shakespeare *say* this owl sounds? When you say, "Tu-whit, tu-who," aloud by itself, does it sound mournful or merry?

When you're out in cold weather, how fast do you move? Is the rhythm of this song slow or quick? If you were singing the song, what mood would your singing express?

At your house, what sounds announce that it is morning?

DAYBREAK ON AVENUE C
(from "The Avenue Bearing the Initial of
Christ into the New World")

pcheek pcheek pcheek pcheek pcheek
They cry. The motherbirds thieve the air
To appease them. A tug on the East River
Blasts the bass-note of its passage, lifted
From the infra-bass of the sea. A broom
Swishes over the sidewalk like feet through leaves.
Valerio's pushcart Ice Coal Kerosene
Moves clack

           clack

             clack
On a broken wheelrim. Ringing in its chains
The New Star Laundry horse comes down the street
Like a roofleak whucking in a pail.
At the redlight, where a horn blares,
The Golden Harvest Bakery brakes on its gears,
Squeaks, and seethes in place. A propane-
gassed bus makes its way with big, airy sighs.

148

Across the street a woman throws open
Her window,
She sets, terribly softly,
Two potted plants on the windowledge
        tic   tic
And bangs shut her window.

A man leaves a doorway tic toc tic toc tic toc tic hurrah
   toc splat on Avenue C tic etc and turns the corner.

Banking the same corner
A pigeon coasts 5th Street in shadows,
Looks for altitude, surmounts the rims of buildings,
And turns white.

The babybirds pipe down. It is day.

—GALWAY KINNELL

Avenue C is a street in New York City. Was this a morning in the 1960's, in 1900, or sometime in between?

Who is crying in the beginning of the poem? What words imitate their cry? What other words in this poem imitate sounds?

Which of the imitated sounds are especially rhythmical? How does the way the lines are printed help suggest some of the rhythms?

What comparisons further suggest the special quality of some of the morning sounds?

How is the rhythm of the pigeon's flight different from the way the man moves?

What kind of day do you think this one will turn out to be?

► ► ►

Have you ever noticed a pet staring at himself in a mirror?
What did he seem to think of his reflection?

THE MONKEY AND THE MIRROR

The Monkey at the mirror saw a Monkey there,
In front of him. He nudged his friend the Bear.
"Just look at that!" he said. "Now, where
On earth did he get such a mug?
How he does smirk and prance about!
If I looked anything at all like that big lout,
I'd hang myself for certain. *Ugh!*

"And yet I must admit
I have some friends who are the spit
And image of that clown. I'll count them. Wait a bit."

"Instead of counting, brother,"
Replied the Bear, "Why don't you look around
Closer to home?" But this advice, though sound,
Went in one monkey's ear and out the other.

—IVAN ANDREEVICH KRYLOV
(translated by Guy Daniels)

Who did the monkey think he saw in the mirror? Did he
like what he saw?

Do you think the bear's advice was sound? Why didn't the
monkey take it?

Does the speech of the monkey and of the bear sound like
ordinary human speech?

What words in the poem make a regular pattern of rhyme?
Do people talking usually rhyme many words?

► ► ►

Herds of antelope may have roamed over Oklahoma before men lived there. Who or what would be an antelope's enemy?

EARTHY ANECDOTE

Every time the bucks went clattering
Over Oklahoma
A firecat bristled in the way.

Wherever they went,
They went clattering,
Until they swerved
In a swift, circular line
To the right,
Because of the firecat.

Or until they swerved
In a swift, circular line
To the left,
Because of the firecat.

The bucks clattered.
The firecat went leaping,
To the right, to the left,
And
Bristled in the way.

Later, the firecat closed his bright eyes
And slept.

—WALLACE STEVENS

What word imitates the sound of the bucks (male antelope)? Why do you suppose the poet described them as roaming over Oklahoma, rather than over some other state?

What do you imagine the firecat to be? In what ways would he be like a fire? In what ways would he be like a cat?

What are the bristles of a brush like? How would the firecat look bristling? How would he sound?

When the bucks swerved, what happened to their movement? How does the sound of *swerve* suit its meaning?

Why do you think the firecat fell asleep? Did he catch an antelope or did he give up? How does the last stanza contrast with the sound of the rest of the poem?

► ► ►

THE KANGAROO

O Kangaroo, O Kangaroo,
Be grateful that you're in the zoo,
And not transmuted by a boomerang
To zestful, tangy Kangaroo meringue.

—OGDEN NASH

► ► ►

What is the purpose of a counting-out rhyme? What kind of
rhythm should it have?

COUNTING-OUT RHYME

Silver bark of beech, and sallow
Bark of yellow birch and yellow
   Twig of willow.

Stripe of green in moosewood maple,
Colour seen in leaf of apple,
   Bark of popple.

Wood of popple pale as moonbeam,
Wood of oak for yoke and barn-beam,
   Wood of hornbeam.

Silver bark of beech, and hollow
Stem of elder, tall and yellow
   Twig of willow.

—EDNA ST. VINCENT MILLAY

   Does a counting-out rhyme necessarily have to make logical
sense? Does this one?
   What do all the things counted in the rhyme have in common?
How are all the colors alike? What mood do the colors suggest
to you?
   Which two stanzas use the same rhyme pattern? Why?

▶ ▶ ▶

Does an old story, like the legend of King Arthur, have a meaning for modern people?

ALL IN GREEN WENT MY LOVE RIDING

All in green went my love riding
on a great horse of gold
into the silver dawn.

four lean hounds crouched low and smiling
the merry deer ran before.

Fleeter be they than dappled dreams
the swift sweet deer
the red rare deer.

Four red roebuck at a white water
the cruel bugle sang before.

Horn at hip went my love riding
riding the echo down
into the silver dawn.

four lean hounds crouched low and smiling
the level meadows ran before.

Softer be they than slippered sleep
the lean lithe deer
the fleet flown deer.

Four fleet does at a gold valley
the famished arrow sang before.

Bow at belt went my love riding
riding the mountain down
into the silver dawn.

four lean hounds crouched low and smiling
the sheer peaks ran before.

Paler be they than daunting death
the sleek slim deer
the tall tense deer.

Four tall stags at a green mountain
the lucky hunter sang before.

All in green went my love riding
on a great horse of gold
into the silver dawn.

four lean hounds crouched low and smiling
my heart fell dead before.

—E. E. CUMMINGS

Does this sound like an old story or a modern one? How did the love who went riding look? What were the colors of the day? Tap out the rhythm of the first two stanzas. What does the rhythm sound like? What initial-letter sounds are repeated in the third stanza?

Each of the first three stanza forms is repeated in the rest of the poem in a regular pattern. But the words are not always exactly the same. Find the stanzas patterned like the first stanza. How are the words varied in these stanzas?

What is the subject of the second stanza? What is the subject of the fourth? How are the two stanzas alike?

Read the second and fourth stanzas and the others patterned like them by themselves. What part of the story do they tell? Why was the arrow that sang before the does *famished*?

Find the other stanzas patterned like the third stanza, and notice the comparisons. In these comparisons, what is happening to the deer?

Do you think a man or a woman is telling this story? According to the last line, who is also being hunted? What do you think "my heart fell dead before" means: that the deer has died, that the speaker has died, or that the speaker has fallen in love?

7

Poems Mean Themselves and Something More

Most poems mean just what they say. For instance, the Midé Indian in "The Sky Clears" beat his drum to make a storm disappear. He hoped that if he beat long enough and in just the right way the sky would clear and the waters become calm.

Most good poems also have outer rings of meaning, just as a pebble dropped into a pond spreads widening rings on the water. The clouds may not actually go away for the Midé Indian, but they may not matter to him any more. The sound of the drum may be so pleasant that he forgets the unpleasantness of the storm. The storm itself might be a real one, but it might be inside the Indian rather than outside. What would the clouds stand for then? What would be happening when the Midé drum sounds?

Like a poem, you usually mean, first of all, exactly what you say. If you say "Thanks" in an ordinary tone of voice, you probably mean it. You might also mean "I like you," even if you don't actually say it. Or perhaps you aren't really grateful. Then you might say "Thanks" and mean just the opposite. What tone of voice would you use?

Sometimes the outer rings of meaning of one poem intersect those of another poem. Then you say that one poem reminds you of another. What poems with similar meanings can you remember? Were the entire poems exactly alike, though? Probably not, because if they were, they'd be the same poem. Even identical twins are two different people, and friends who know them well can tell them apart.

Each poem is, like you, an individual. You may wear clothes very much like everyone else's. You may be taking the same subjects as many other students. You may use the same expressions your friends do. Your telephone voice may even sound almost as if someone else is speaking, perhaps another member of your family. But you are you; there is no one else exactly like you. In the same way, each poem is unique.

In reading a poem, the first thing to do is to listen to it as carefully as you'd like someone to listen to you when you're saying something important. After you've heard what the poem is saying, then you can think about it. What else might it mean? Why might different people in your class have different ideas about additional meanings?

Finally, if you compare a poem with one it reminds you of, you may discover further meanings that they have in common. At the same time, you can also hear the individual poems more distinctly than you did before.

I, TOO

I, too, sing America.

I am the darker brother.
They send me to eat in the kitchen
When company comes,
But I laugh,
And eat well,
And grow strong.

Tomorrow,
I'll sit at the table
When company comes.
Nobody'll dare
Say to me,
"Eat in the kitchen,"
Then.

Besides,
They'll see how beautiful I am
And be ashamed—

I, too, am America.

—LANGSTON HUGHES

What difference does it seem to make to the speaker where he eats? Why might he think "they" will be ashamed?

From what other places, besides the table, might the same speaker be excluded? Where else, besides at the table, might he expect to sit tomorrow?

How does a botanist tell one tree from another?

THE PLUM-TREE

The back-yard has a tiny plum-tree,
It shows how small a tree can be.
Yet there it is, railed round
So no one tramps it to the ground.

It's reached its full shape, low and meagre.
O yes, it wants to grow more, it's eager
For what can't be done—
It gets too little sun.

A plum-tree no hand's ever been at
To pick a plum: it strains belief.
It is a plum-tree for all that—
We know it by the leaf.

—BERTOLT BRECHT
(translated by Edwin Morgan)

How does the speaker in the poem know that the tree is a plum tree?

Sometimes the roots and branches of a tree are trimmed on purpose to keep the tree small. Is that what's happened to this tree? Do you think anyone cares about the tree?

Are people ever prevented from growing, as the plum tree has been? In what ways might they be prevented?

Why do astronomers study stars? Why do people stargaze?

WHEN I HEARD THE LEARN'D ASTRONOMER

When I heard the learn'd astronomer,
When the proofs, the figures, were ranged in columns
    before me,
When I was shown the charts and diagrams, to add, divide,
    and measure them,
When I sitting heard the astronomer where he lectured with
    much applause in the lecture-room,
How soon unaccountable I became tired and sick,
Till rising and gliding out I wander'd off by myself,
In the mystical moist night-air, and from time to time,
Look'd up in perfect silence at the stars.

—WALT WHITMAN

Why do you think Walt Whitman became tired of the lecture?
Would you have joined him in wandering off?

THE TERM

A rumpled sheet
of brown paper
about the length

and apparent bulk
of a man was
rolling with the

wind slowly over
and over in
the street as

a car drove down
upon it and
crushed it to

the ground. Unlike
a man it rose
again rolling

with the wind over
and over to be as
it was before.

—WILLIAM CARLOS WILLIAMS

How did the paper look like a man? How was it unlike a man?
How long is a *term* at your school? What is usually considered
to be the full term of a man's life? What would happen if a car
crushed a man like a sheet of paper?

Do you think the title refers to a man's life term, to the life
term of a sheet of paper, or to both?

► ► ►

163

What is extraordinary about a flying fish?

FLYING FISH

I have lived in many half-worlds myself . . . and so I know
    you.

I leaned at a deck rail watching a monotonous sea, the same
    circling birds and the same plunge of furrows carved
    by the plowing keel.

I leaned so . . . and you fluttered struggling between two
    waves in the air now . . . and then under the water and out
    again . . . a fish . . . a bird . . . a fin thing . . . a wing thing.

Child of water, child of air, fin thing and wing thing . . .
    I have lived in many half-worlds myself . . . and so I
    know you.

—CARL SANDBURG

How does the speaker feel about the flying fish? Why does
he feel that way?

What was the speaker doing when the flying fish appeared?
What made the sea monotonous? What is the keel of the boat
compared to? When could plowing be monotonous? How does
the rhythm of the second stanza fit the description of the sea?

How did the flying fish move in the air? Why can't you tell
how he moved in the water?

What do you think the fish is doing in the pauses marked,
". . ."? What might the man be doing in the pauses? What would
be the movement of the boat?

What words in the third stanza are repeated in the fourth? What pattern of sound connects these words to each other? What line from another stanza is repeated? What new idea is added?

What half-worlds might people live in? For example, as a student you live in the school world. But that world isn't your entire world. What worlds do you live in outside of school? Why might the worlds you live in be called "half-worlds," even though there are more than two halves?

Which world does the flying fish seem to be more comfortable in? Why might it seem that he is more comfortable there? Does it seem easy to live in many half-worlds?

▶ ▶ ▶

WHO HAS SEEN THE WIND?

A Spanish sculptor named Cherino
Has seen the wind.
He says it is shaped like a coil of hardened copper
And spirals into itself and out again,
That it is very heavy
And can break your toe if it falls on your foot.
Be careful when you are moving the wind,
It can put you in the hospital!

—BOB KAUFMAN

Does the wind usually blow continuously in the same direction? What do you think suggested a spiral for the shape of the wind?

Sometimes people talk about the winds of change. If you were trying to change something, would you need to be as careful as if you were moving Cherino's statue?

▶ ▶ ▶

A mockingbird has no song of his own. He imitates all the sounds he hears.

THE MOCKINGBIRD

Look one way and the sun is going down,
Look the other and the moon is rising.
The sparrow's shadow's longer than the lawn.
The bats squeak: "Night is here," the birds cheep:
    "Day is gone."
On the willow's highest branch, monopolizing
Day and night, cheeping, squeaking, soaring,
The mockingbird is imitating life.

All day the mockingbird has owned the yard.
As light first woke the world, the sparrows trooped
Onto the seedy lawn: the mockingbird
Chased them off shrieking. Hour by hour, fighting hard
To make the world his own, he swooped
On thrushes, thrashers, jays, and chickadees—
At noon he drove away a big black cat.

Now, in the moonlight, he sits here and sings.
A thrush is singing, then a thrasher, then a jay—
Then, all at once, a cat begins meowing.
A mockingbird can sound like anything.
He imitates the world he drove away
So well that for a minute, in the moonlight,
Which one's the mockingbird? which one's the world?

—RANDALL JARRELL

When does the mockingbird sing? Why do you think he waits until then?

What words in the poem imitate sounds, as the mockingbird imitates the animals?

In the story of *The Bat-Poet*, the chipmunk liked this poem when the bat poet said it for him. But the chipmunk was sure the mockingbird wouldn't like it. And the mockingbird didn't. He was angry, insisting that nobody had any idea how much all the animals got on his nerves. How would you sum up the mockingbird's personality?

Do you think the bat poet wrote this poem to criticize the mockingbird? Which world do you think is the real world: the one the bat and chipmunk saw and heard, or the world in the mockingbird's songs?

► ► ►

Sometimes logging companies would clean out all the trees in a forest. Only stumps were left standing. To get the timber out to the main roads, the loggers paved rough skidroads with split logs (puncheon).

BERRY-PICKING
(Poem 6 from *Logging*)

"In that year, 1914, we lived on the farm
And the relatives lived with us.
A banner year for wild blackberries
Dad was crazy about wild blackberries
No berries like that now.
You know Kitsap County was logged before
The turn of the century—it was easiest of all,
Close to water, virgin timber,
When I was a kid walking about in the
Stumpland, wherever you'd go a skidroad
Puncheon, all overgrown.
We went up one like that, fighting our way through
To its end near the top of a hill:
For some reason wild blackberries
Grew best there. We took off one morning
Right after milking: rode the horses
To a valley we'd been to once before
Hunting berries, and hitched the horses.
About a quarter mile up the old road
We found the full ripe of berrytime—
And with only two pails—so we
Went back home, got Mother and Ruth,
And filled lots of pails. Mother sent letters
To all the relatives in Seattle:
Effie, Aunt Lucy, Bill Moore,
Forrest, Edna, six or eight, they all came

Out to the farm, and we didn't take pails
Then: we took copper clothes-boilers,
Wash-tubs, buckets, and all went picking.
We were canning for three days."

—GARY SNYDER

Why do you think this poem is in quotation marks?

A logged-out forest can be a very sad place. Can you imagine why? Does the Stumpland described in this poem seem to be deserted or full of life?

What did they have to do to get to the berries? Why do you think the best blackberries grew at the top? Often, where are the best things?

Is *ripe* usually an adjective or a noun? Which is it in the poem? How does "the full ripe of berrytime" make you see a picture different from the one you would see if the poem said, "ripe berries"?

Why did they have only two pails the first time they found the berries? What did they end up doing? Do things sometimes start out the way this berry-picking did? Do they sometimes end this way?

▶ ▶ ▶

Cattle often try to get through a fence to an identical field on the other side. Why do you think they try?

WIRES

The widest prairies have electric fences,
For though old cattle know they must not stray,
Young steers are always scenting purer water
Not here but anywhere. Beyond the wires

Leads them to blunder up against the wires
Whose muscle-shredding violence gives no quarter.
Young steers become old cattle from that day,
Electric limits to their widest senses.

—PHILIP LARKIN

Why do these fields have electric fences? How do the fences work?

Can you think of any other way the young steers might learn? How desirable would this kind of education be for you?

▶ ▶ ▶

In Paris and other European cities, the final step in opening a window is to open the outside wooden shutters.

THIS MORNING

This morning I threw the windows
of my room open, the light burst
in like crystal gauze and I hung
it on my wall to frame.
And here I am watching it take possession
of my room, watching the obscure love
match of light and shadow—of cold and warmth.
It is a matter of acceptance, I guess.
It is a matter of finding some room
with shadows to embrace, open. Now
the light has settled in, I don't think
I shall ever close my windows again.

—JAY WRIGHT

Why is the light so welcome in the room?

Sometimes people shut out other kinds of enlightenment, such as being aware of how someone else feels. Once you have become aware of how others feel and think, do you think you'd ever want to close the windows of your understanding again?

I scooped up the moon
In my water
Bucket . . . and
Spilled it on the grass

—RYUHO

What did Ryuho spill on the grass? Do you think he spilled it by accident or on purpose? How would the grass look?

When do children playing hide and seek call, "Come out, come out, wherever you arc"?

HIDE AND SEEK
(an Easter ballad)

"Come OUT, come OUT, wherEVer you are,"
The frisking children chorused.
　　When playtime ends,
　　All hidden friends
Are bound to come out of the forest.

"Come OUT, come OUT, wherEVer you are,"
The tidy children chorused,
　　In the short proud street
　　Where our lives are neat
On the nearer side of the forest.

"Come OUT, come OUT, wherEVer you are,"
The puzzled children chorused.
　　When fun is over,
　　Why doesn't the rover
Come whooping out of the forest?

"Come OUT, come OUT, wherEVer you are,"
The lonely children chorused;
　　For the greater the dark
　　The less the lark
When you wait till dusk near a forest.

"Come OUT, come OUT, wherEVer you are,"
The shivering children chorused.
(With some wonderful toy
Can't we tug back the boy
Who is westering into the forest?)

"Come OUT, come OUT, wherEVer you are,"
We aging children chorused —
While beyond our shout
A boy comes out
On the farther side of the forest.

— PETER VIERECK

Why doesn't the boy answer the children?

What word describes the children in the first stanza? In the other stanzas? What do the last three lines of all stanzas (except the last) show about how the children feel?

How does the way the children feel change? Until the fifth stanza the boy they call is invisible. Then his disappearance is suddenly explained. Do you think the children know why the boy has disappeared?

What kind of people have gone "westering" in the United States? How can someone be a pioneer today? What might the boy be doing?

In the second line of the last stanza, why do you suppose the poet changed "The" to "We"? How can people be both *aging* and *children*? What keeps the boy still a boy?

▶ ▶ ▶

Would stories of magic be more likely to happen in sunlight or in moonlight?

THE SONG OF WANDERING AENGUS

I went out to the hazel wood,
Because a fire was in my head,
And cut and peeled a hazel wand,
And hooked a berry to a thread;
And when white moths were on the wing,
And moth-like stars were flickering out,
I dropped the berry in a stream
And caught a little silver trout.

When I had laid it on the floor
I went to blow the fire aflame,
But something rustled on the floor,
And some one called me by my name:
It had become a glimmering girl
With apple blossom in her hair
Who called me by my name and ran
And faded through the brightening air.

Though I am old with wandering
Through hollow lands and hilly lands,
I will find out where she has gone,
And kiss her lips and take her hands;
And walk among long dappled grass,
And pluck till time and times are done
The silver apples of the moon,
The golden apples of the sun.

—WILLIAM BUTLER YEATS

At what time of day did Aengus catch his fish? What would make stars look moth-like? What is the main color in the first stanza?

How might a trout seem to change into a girl? What was she like? What time of day is it by the end of the second stanza?

How long has Aengus searched for her? What expected rewards still lead him on? Do you think he will ever find her?

Do people ever spend their entire lives searching for something, without ever finding it? Why do they keep trying?

► ► ►

What is a jellyfish like? Would you like to touch a live one?

A JELLYFISH

Visible, invisible,
   a fluctuating charm
an amber-tinctured amethyst
   inhabits it, your arm
approaches and it opens
   and it closes; you had meant
to catch it and it quivers;
   you abandon your intent.

                —MARIANNE MOORE

Why do people build fences around their houses?

A FENCE

Now the stone house on the lake front is finished and the
   workmen are beginning the fence.
The palings are made of iron bars with steel points that
   can stab the life out of any man who falls on them.
As a fence, it is a masterpiece, and will shut off the rabble
   and all vagabonds and hungry men and all wandering
   children looking for a place to play.
Passing through the bars and over the steel points will go
   nothing except Death and the Rain and Tomorrow.

—CARL SANDBURG

Would you like to live in a house surrounded by a fence like
this? What is the purpose of this fence? Is it a good fence?

What will be able to go through and over the fence? Why
might Sandburg think they'll be able to get by the fence? Do you
agree with his thought?

► ► ►

How can a poem seem alive, like a person or an animal?

THE POEM

It discovers by night
what the day hid from it.
Sometimes it turns itself
into an animal.
In summer it takes long walks
by itself where meadows
fold back from ditches.
Once it stood still
in a quiet row of machines.
Who knows
what it is thinking?

—DONALD HALL

Sometimes during the day, things happen so quickly that it's impossible to find time to think about them. How could you discover at night what you couldn't understand during the day?

Imagine an animal-like poem. Would it be likely to make you think deeply? Would it make pleasant or unpleasant sounds?

Why do people enjoy taking long walks by themselves? Where and when would a poem enjoy walking? What rhythm would a walking poem have?

Are poems often about machines? What would a poem be likely to say about machines, even about quiet machines?

Do you think a poem thinks? If it does, who knows what the poems you have read are thinking? Do you think the poet knows? Do you know?

► ► ►

SOUTHERN MANSION

Poplars are standing there still as death
And ghosts of dead men
Meet their ladies walking
Two by two beneath the shade
And standing on the marble steps.

There is a sound of music echoing
Through the open door
And in the field there is
Another sound tinkling in the cotton:
Chains of bondmen dragging on the ground.

The years go back with an iron clank,
A hand is on the gate,
A dry leaf trembles on the wall.
Ghosts are walking.
They have broken roses down
And poplars stand there still as death.

—ARNA BONTEMPS

What was life like for the gentlemen and ladies who lived in the Southern mansion? What was life like for the bondmen?

Do you think the poet describes the people as ghosts because they have come back to haunt the mansion, or because they never really lived even while they were alive, or for both reasons?

THE SPECTACLES

Korf reads avidly and fast.
Therefore he detests the vast
bombast of the repetitious,
twelvefold needless, injudicious.

Most affairs are settled straight
just in six words or in eight;
in as many tapeworm phrases
one can prattle on like blazes.

Hence he lets his mind invent
a corrective instrument:
Spectacles whose focal strength
shortens texts of any length.

Thus, a poem such as this,
so beglassed one would just—miss.
Thirty-three of them will spark
nothing but one question mark.

—CHRISTIAN MORGENSTERN
(translated by Max Knight)

179

THE SLEEPER

When I was the sissy of the block who nobody
    wanted on their team
Sonny Hugg persisted in believing that my small size
    was an asset
Not the liability and curse I felt it was
And he saw a use for my swift feet with which I ran
    away from fights.

He kept putting me into complicated football plays
Which would have been spectacular if they worked:
For instance, me getting clear in front and him
    shooting the ball over—
Or the sensation of the block, the Sleeper Play
In which I would lie down on the sidelines near the
    goal
As though resting and out of action, until the scrim-
    mage began
And I would step onto the field, receive the long
    throw
And to the astonishment of all the tough guys in the
    world
Step over the goal line for a touchdown.

That was the theory anyway. In practice
I had the fatal flaw of not being able to catch
And usually had my fingers bent back and the
    breath knocked out of me
So the plays always failed, but Sonny kept on trying
Until he grew up out of my world into the glamorous
Varsity crowd, the popular kids of Lynbrook High.

But I will always have this to thank him for:
That when I look back on childhood
(That four psychiatrists haven't been able to help
    me bear the thought of)
There is not much to be glad for
Besides his foolish and delicious faith
That, with all my oddities, there was a place in the
    world for me
If only he could find the special role.

                    —EDWARD FIELD

relish radishes

the food of life
is a bite of itself

                    —ROBERT K. HALL

A PICTURE

A little
house with
small
windows,

a gentle
fall of the
ground to
a small

stream. The trees
are both close
and green, a tall
sense of enclosure.

There is a sky
of blue
and a faint sun
through clouds.

—ROBERT CREELEY

If you were illustrating this poem-picture, what mood would you want your illustration to suggest?

UNNATURAL, UNUSUAL AND UNFAIR

Eroded beach on the bay, an empty scene,
Only an old Negro lady hunched in her coat,
Hermit-shaped, at the end of a narrow,
moss-green wharf fishing—

A bundle of fog binding her together
With shore, sailboat, and a black buoy
Like a period mark in an unnatural sentence.

A sense of bungled weather, bullheaded sky,
But out of a ripple, action! Honeymoon of hook
And a hornpipe in her homely face,
Climbs dripping her kitchen cord line
And what she hooks is unusual—

Lean leopard shark, small, yellow lefthander
With a blasted eye at his hoity-toity family tree.
Back sinks the scene to its bungled sense,
Hollowhearted, unsuccessful, and unfair.

—JAMES SCHEVILL

What would a natural fishing scene look like? What is unnatural
about this one?

How does the lady show her feelings about hooking the fish?
A leopard shark is an important food fish in California. Will this
particular shark furnish much food?

Do you usually think of eating sharks? What might be unfair
about the life a leopard shark has to lead, compared to other mem-
bers of the shark family?

What other parts of the lady's life might be unnatural, unusual,
or unfair?

183

BOY WITH A HARE

In fall light
and the highway,
a child
holding up in his hands
not lanterns
or petals
but the death of a hare.

Motorcars rake
the cold causeways.
Faces are glazed
under
windshields,
eyeballs
of metal
and inimical
ears,
teeth hurrying,
crackling their lightning,
sheering away to the sea and the cities;
and a child
with a hare
in the autumn,
shy
as a
thistle seed,
rigid
as flint,
lifting
his hand
to the
fume
of the motorcade.

Nobody
slackens.

It is tawny
up on the ridges,
on the summit,
the hues
of a puma, pursued.
The silence
goes
violet.
Like
cinders, black diamonds,
the eyes
of the child and the hare,
two
knife-points
upright
on a knifeblade,
two little black poniards,
the eyes
of a little child
lost,
who
proffers
the death of a hare
in the towering
fall
of the road.

—PABLO NERUDA
(translated by Ben Belitt)

Why do you think the child is standing by the highway, holding
up the dead hare? How are the child and the hare different from
the motorcars and the people in them?

Do birds fly more easily with or against the wind?

THE MANOEUVRE

I saw the two starlings
coming in toward the wires.
But at the last,
just before alighting, they

turned in the air together
and landed backwards!
that's what got me—to
face into the wind's teeth.

—WILLIAM CARLOS WILLIAMS

What would the two starlings look like together? Why do you suppose they landed backwards?

What "got" the poet? Why? What is a wind with "teeth" like? What would it take to face into such a wind?

What winds with teeth do people sometimes have to face? What kind of people face such winds? Why do you think they do it? Do they do it better alone or with someone else?

► ► ►

When you waken and look out the window, what might make you laugh?

I TRY TO WAKEN AND GREET THE WORLD ONCE AGAIN

In a pine tree,
A few yards away from my window sill,
A brilliant blue jay is springing up and down, up and down,
On a branch.
I laugh, as I see him abandon himself
To entire delight, for he knows as well as I do
That the branch will not break.

—JAMES WRIGHT

Why won't branches break? What are you quite sure will not break?

190

193